First printing April 2023

Library of Congress Cataloging-in-Publication Data

Paperback ISBN: 9798387648854
Hardcover ISBN: 9798387648960

Assilian, Ara H.
pearls of life: reflections of faith, hope and love while facing life's challenges / by Ara H. Assilian

Published by AR PRESS, an American Real Publishing Company
Roger L. Brooks, Publisher
roger@americanrealpublishing.com
americanrealpublishing.com

Edited by Claire Gault
Interior design by Eva Myrick
Cover design by AR PRESS

Printed in the U.S.A.

PEARLS OF LIFE

**Reflections of Faith, Hope and Love
While Facing Life's Challenges**

Ara H. Assilian

This book is dedicated to the life of my second son, Hrag Assilian, 1979-1992

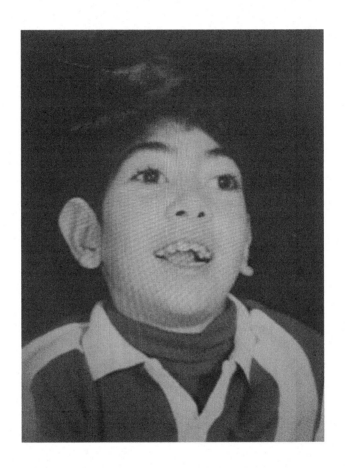

TABLE OF CONTENTS

SECTION V PEARLS OF FAMILY AND LOVE.................217

SECTION I

PEARLS OF LIFE

PEARLS OF LIFE

Pearls are formed

When a natural irritant

Works its way into an oyster, mussel, or clam.

As a defensive mechanism,

A fluid coats the irritant.

Layer upon layer, this coating called 'nacre'

Is deposited until a lustrous pearl is formed.

In certain ways,

Human beings are just like oysters,

Glued on the beaches of life's thundering ocean.

Ferocious waves hit the shores constantly;

Thunderstorms and hurricanes occasionally bring cataclysmic destruction,

And the oyster takes the hits.

Clamps down hard,

Tumbles up and down on the rocks,

And converts all the irritations it receives,

Into a sparkling pearl.

The more ferocious the storms,

The glossier the pearl becomes.

This book of poetry is the result of life's constant irritations,

Life's constant ups and downs,

The pain, anguish, suffering, hopelessness, despair, depression,
failures, tears and pain,

Are mixed with unshakeable faith, love, achievement, success and
harmony,

Generating flawless pearls throughout our lives.

In the end,

We can gaze at the stunning hues of the pearls we have created,

And enjoy the beauty of God's awe-inspiring creation.

The pearls of our life.

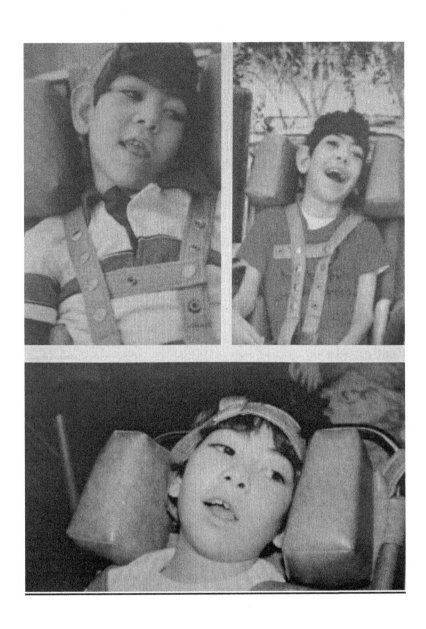

PRICELESS ETERNITY

Back when my second son Hrag was alive,

I remember a family outing to the local mall,

With my wife, my first son Shahe, and Hrag,

I tenderly placed my handicapped son in his special stroller,

And walked through the mall, window-shopping.

As we proceeded from one shop to another,

Suddenly my son started experiencing his occasional seizures,

Which would happen with no prior indication or notice,

During which he uncontrollably throws his head backward, his
eyes rolling back,

His arms and legs became very stiff like a rock.

He jerked around with no control.

Right at that moment, four to five kids were walking by from the
opposite direction,

They fully noticed my son's abnormal behavior,

And one of them quipped, "Look at that freaky kid,"

That careless comment from a young boy,

With no knowledge of his circumstances and medical condition,

Was a sharp dagger slicing my heart in two.

For those kids, seeing my son in a funny-looking stroller,

Having seizures with eyes turning white,

Was not something they witnessed every day.

I grabbed my son's palms to calm him down,

I put him on my lap, squeezed him to my chest, and sobbed.

That was the last time I dared to take him to a mall.

Esther continued taking him out by herself after that; she was like a granite rock,

But the pain was too unbearable for me.

Funny, for those kids, my son was a "freak."

For me, my son was the best thing I have ever done, or will ever do;

He was my living angel.

Angels are divine, sinless creatures,

Our human brain is the center of our sinful nature,

That's where our self-awareness, self-interest,

Self-enrichment and selfishness are born.

Most of my son's brain cells died the day he was born;

So accordingly, he is the only sinless human being that I have met.

Hrag's brain, as he was birthed,

In self actions that are so difficult to imagine and comprehend,

Every time the attending nurse asked my wife to push,

With my wife's umbilical cords wrapped tightly around my son's neck,

His oxygen intake was partially blocked for some thirty minutes.

She pushed to deliver a new life, but unknowingly suffocated our own son

The painful delivery process led to 75% of Hrag's brain cells dying.

Right before delivery,

A fully-grown, over nine pounds beautiful baby emerged

With the most amazing eyelashes.

To this day, I have never been able to understand and accept

Where was God?

A new human being was being born,

And for reasons unbeknownst to me, our Creator was absent.

He was not there for Hrag right at the beginning of his life.

As such, my son was the only sinless person I knew and have met,

He indeed was my heavenly angel,

He was my divine sinless creature,

So many times, I remember putting him in my lap,

Putting my thumb in his little hand,

And looking at his big, black visionless eyes.

I could see and feel the presence of the Holy Spirit,

Through his beautiful smiling eyes,

In my son's bedroom.

Those moments: the warmth, comfort, and essence of pure love,

Build up my priceless eternity.

If the Holy Spirit was absent during delivery, I sure felt His presence,

During the thirteen years of Hrag's life.

(Which, according to delivery doctors, was only supposed to be a day or two.)

"Look at that freaky kid" from a passerby, young teenager,

Was indeed referring to my son,

Who, for me, was a peek toward priceless eternity.

May 2021

WHEN NO ONE CAN CONSOLE

Few of us are fortunate in our lifetime

To experience events or accidents that no one in our surroundings can console.

Parents, relatives, friends, doctors, pastors, parishioners,

All become speechless.

They typically would have no experience or understanding

Of what you are going through.

Accordingly, their input and advice becomes useless or irrelevant.

It was such an experience that I went through with my wife,

During the birth of our second son,

Who was born accidently asphyxiated during the last stages of delivery.

Suddenly we were face to face with tragedy on one of our supposed happiest days,

It turned into a thirteen years' nightmare and consolation.

A beautiful, nine-and-a-half pounds, fully grown baby was welcome to this world,

With only the inner center part of his brain still intact:

The one that controls his breathing, heartbeat, and blood circulation,

Almost all of the outer brain compartments/cells that control other essential functions,

Like seeing, hearing, moving, walking, learning, eating, talking, and so on, were destroyed

Due to the lack of oxygen during the last phase of childbirth.

Doctors told us that due to the malfunctioning of various organs of our son, Hrag

(Which means "little fire" in Armenian.)

He would live only a day or two,

Miraculously, he lived for thirteen years.

A few days after he was born, they told us his future was hopeless

And asked our permission to stop all preventative measures and disconnect

All life-sustaining tubes and wires connected to our son's motionless body,

My answer was that God gave us a son,

Let Him decide what to do,

That night, the doctors disconnected all the wires and tubes,

And we went home from the hospital wondering who do we had to call

For a white casket for our son.

Next morning, the hospital called,

And they informed that Hrag was breathing by himself,

His collapsed lung was now functioning normally.

His liver, which was under severe stress, seemed to be okay.

Within two weeks, they allowed us to bring him home.

Months and years passed,

And we learned things about our human brain we have never bothered to know or inquired before.

Many parts of human organs and cells regrow when damaged,

But when a brain cell dies they are gone for good.

We have seen so many doctors, therapists, spiritual healers,

I have searched my inner soul praying, seeking a miracle from God,

To save and bring hope, to bring life to my son.

As the years passed, with great uncertainty but daring courage,

We decided to have another child, and Lara was born,

Our friends and relatives, seeing the amount of time

We were devoting to Hrag, counseled us to institutionalize Hrag.

So that we can focus our energy on our two healthy children

We wouldn't hear any arguments like that,

Even though they told us it would effect Shahe and Lara,

When they see week after week that

Their parents would spend a lot more time with Hrag.

My response was consistent,

They all are from my blood.

With no hesitation, I would show the same commitment and love,

To any one of them, knowing full well

That my healthy children will eventually understand

That I had no favoritism.

Hrag simply was incapable of doing anything by himself,

We had to do everything for him, twenty-four hours every day for
thirteen years.

Naturally caring for our second son

Became a cornerstone of our life,

A soul-searching journey to understand the meaning of life.

To redefine loving, as only God loves us; one way.

Where thank you is not required,

Every moment, hour, day, weak and month,

We had to think about what our son needs and then provide it to him with love.

Just like our God does to each one of us every day, with no expectation,

When I learned about God's immense, boundless love,

What better consolation do I need?

I found the Consoler in Chief,

I FOUND GOD'S LOVE.

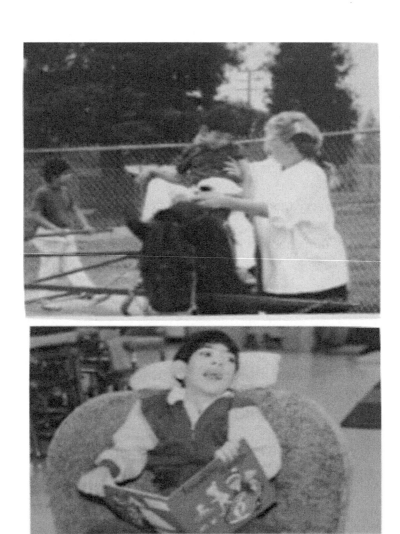

what a smile. I sure am cute!

TO MY SPECIAL SON

My son, the holiest of living souls, smile,

Since in your tender and shiny face,

You reflect the purest of innocent love,

For God, for reasons known only to him,

Has blessed you with eyes, but you cannot see the beauty of this world,

Ears, but you cannot hear the songs of thousand birds,

Legs, but you cannot climb mountains of heaven,

Hands, but you cannot write the poetry swirling in your mind,

Lips, but you cannot kiss your loved ones all around

Tongue, but you cannot sing the songs of your heart,

And brain, oh yes, a brain that has left you lifeless and motionless,

At an age when you are supposed to jump all over,

With your brother, sister, mother, and me,

Running together, learning, dancing, playing and praying earnestly together.

Yes, my son, all these you cannot do, but you smile, and I know that,

God is smiling through you,

Telling us to wait,

Till your living will have a meaning one day,

And we will all be there, to witness and hail.

March 28th, 1987

NEXT TO MY SON'S HOSPITAL BED

My dearest God,

Possessor of my inner soul,

Here we are all alone, you, my son, and I.

Fill this room with your Holy presence,

And your almighty power of love.

Oh my God,

With Your sacred presence in this room, tell me, please: why?

Why do you test the strength of my belief?

Why, my Lord, do you force me to question your reason?

For depriving my son of all the worldly joys,

For depriving him of life in this world,

Which I am sure he would have lived,

As a model believer in your righteousness.

Why my Lord, did you strike a human being,

Who, for me, personifies the purest of angels above,

For he has endured with love,

Continuous suffering from the day he was born.

Tell me then, my Lord: Why?

You must have a good reason, enlighten my mind and soul,

To see Your aim for my son.

February 28th, 1984

IT'S MY TURN TO FEED

One early evening, I returned home from Citibank,

Still in my banker's vested suit.

I noticed my wife was feeding my son Hrag.

She had him on her lap, almost 4 ½ feet tall,

Feeding him the healthy liquefied food that she usually prepares
for him.

I noticed Hrag was having his occasional seizures,

During which he turns very stiff,

Both arms and legs sticking straight out with extreme tension,

With his head pulling back and down on Esther's left arm.

In exasperation, Esther said she couldn't feed him any more, she
was too exhausted,

The constant pressure on her left arm was causing severe pain in
her lower back.

So, having just arrived from my office at the right time,

I volunteered:

"It's my turn to feed."

I took off my suit jacket,

Carefully put him on my lap and continued the feeding process.

"Maybe he already had enough," I said,

"No way, that is his nutrition. You have to finish the whole dish," she retorted emphatically.

So, in obedience I continued.

My son cannot chew nor swallow his food;

You have to move his chin up and down, with the hope of gradually directing the food to his throat.

Many times the liquefied food ended up in his lungs, which required constant hospitalization.

He also cannot respond or tell us he had enough.

This feeding process typically takes sixty to ninety minutes.

Naturally Esther does it a lot faster than me,

When I was two-thirds done, I told Esther that I thought he was full,

He didn't want it any more.

"That's his nutrition, you have to finish the whole plate," She screamed from the adjacent kitchen.,

So, I obediently continued with one, two more spoonfuls,

And then like a volcano, Hrag coughed and vomited everything he had in his belly,

Crying uncontrollably,

The food was thrown everywhere, on the couch I was sitting on,

On my suit, on the floor, all over his body,

In an upset moment, I left him in a clean section of the couch

"Why did you do that?" I inquired.

He was crying uncontrollably.

I immediately realized my stupidity.

Why am I asking him? He doesn't know why?

It was just his physical body reaction telling us he had enough,

Or some food was going to his lungs instead of stomach.

I immediately stopped worrying about cleaning up the mess,

Held him on my chest, and started crying with him

"I'm sorry, I'm sorry, I know, you don't know what you are doing,

Mummy wanted you to finish your meal, I should have stopped

It's okay, it's okay," I said, trying to calm him down.

That was a normal welcome back home from work.

Now, try to mentally understand the fate of your son,

And what your wife goes through all day.

The mental, physical, emotional unbearable stress.

Can you see any light? Any hope?

AN ANGEL HAS DEPARTED

My living angel has left.

He peacefully went at night to join the Lord,

Just before his thirteenth birthday.

And what a privilege it was to have him as a son,

To have the honor and glory of caring for a saint.

My son was destined to be in bed, for all his life.

He never learned or said a word,

He never walked, talked, or wrote anything.

In our human eyes and thoughts, he never accomplished or did anything

of any significance.

But in God's eyes,

He will be my wife's and my greatest achievement that we have ever made,

or that we will ever make for the rest of our lives.

For God, through our son, gave a glimpse of His immeasurable love to us,

He taught us the meaning of everlasting and unconditional love, care, and

commitment.

No matter how difficult the circumstances happen to be,

Till death do us part.

For this Godly insight, we thank our Lord.

We are deeply saddened by the loss of our son,

Our living angel,

For he left without realization of my greatest dream.

Which was the belief that one day,

my son would hug me and tell me

I love you, Dad,

I love you, Mom,

But I know he can say it now.

He is saying, "I love you, mom and dad" right at this very moment,

Up in heaven.

And one day when we join him, he will give us that pleasure and honor in person,

In the Divine presence of our Lord.

May God give him peace and happiness during his everlasting life.

March 21st, 1992

SEND ME MORE PAIN & SUFFERING

Our scripture reading last Sunday

From James 1; 2-4.

It brought beautiful memories for me, reading,

"Consider it pure joy, my brothers,

Whenever you face trials of many kinds,

Because you know that testing of your faith, develops
perseverance,

Perseverance must finish its work,

So that you mature and complete, not lacking anything."

Naturally, when we go through trials and difficulties,

The last thing we think about is the feeling of joy.

Usually, we cry out, "Why me, Lord?"

But I distinctly remember,

When my second son was alive for thirteen years,

Severely handicapped, in constant pain,

Unable to walk, see, hear, and eat

living like a vegetable

With constant soul-wrenching hospital stays throughout his living life,

I used to pray:

"Lord, do You have more pain and suffering?

Send them my way, because

The higher the level of pain, the closer I get to You."

I know it is ironic and difficult to comprehend,

But if you have gone through severe pain,

You know exactly what I am talking about.

The feeling of being so close to our Lord

Is an eternal joy that you will experience,

When you know for sure, that He will never forsake you.

No matter how difficult your circumstances are.

Embrace the pain and the resulting healing you will receive.

HOW WILL YOU FACE?

Thump . . . thump . . . thump . . .

Do you feel your heartbeat?

Press your thumb and point finger together.

Do you feel your pulse ticking?

If you do, thank God you're alive.

Many who felt the same yesterday,

Don't feel anything today,

Because their heart stopped ticking, stopped pumping.

I know we never think death will happen to us,

We are young, we eat right, we exercise,

We have a close-knit family, we love God,

We feel we are "protected."

Dying is not for us,

It's not on our planned agenda,

And never crosses our minds.

But suddenly, we get a close call,

A favorite relative, friend, dear neighbor, or an associate,

Who was younger and healthier than us.

What happened? How did it happen? How could it be?

That they are no longer with us.

You were just with them yesterday,

You laughed, talked, planned future outings together,

And today they are gone.

I've seen and felt this around me several times,

Who would be next? You wonder.

When is my turn coming? You ponder.

When my parents, son, relatives, and close friends departed from this world,

I've sustained these experiences with complete peace,

Because when I was actually tested during a live earthquake,

While almost all were panicked,

I was engulfed with the presence of the Holy Spirit.

I was joyful and ready to see my angelic son,

Who has departed way before his "normal" time,

Who was waiting for me on the other side.

I had no anxiety about death;

I had a pleasant anticipation

Of a new and happy beginning.

How will you face yours?

When death stares you in the eye.

Will it be the beginning of eternal life? The choice is yours to make.

ONE DAY AT A TIME

Sometimes we get hit in life,

With a major catastrophic accident or

A horrible life-changing event,

With long-term and painful consequences,

Promising continuous suffering for years to come.

Or, in some cases, for the rest of our lives.

How can we overcome the unbearable daily pain?

How can we gather ourselves to create inner willpower and energy?

To fight, sustain, persevere against all difficulties,

That hit us so suddenly, with no prior notice,

No warning, no alarming signals,

Keeping us in a daze and confused about what to do next?

How to have the energy to wake up and face tomorrow's unbearable challenges?

Life suddenly has lost its meaning and luster,

The more we look at our current circumstances,

The more we get depressed with the weight of it all.

Will there be an end to this misery?

Oh yes, there will be an end.

The Lord knows exactly how much we can bear,

And He will never give us more than what we can handle.

You will be surprised at the level of your resiliency,

The process usually starts when you learn to take all the pain you are facing.

One simple day at a time,

Just focus on making it through today,

Gather enough energy and courage to survive;

The sun will rise again tomorrow and will bring a new day.

You will face tomorrow's problems tomorrow,

ONE DAY AT A TIME.

OVERCOMING DEPRESSION

You sit at the edge of your bed.

You can't sleep,

Too scared to close your eyes,

With no energy to stand on your own feet.

Besides, even if you close your eyes, you feel haunted by nightmares,

The mental and emotional stress is just unbearable,

From so many places, all coming for you at the same time,

The emotional weight of your son's hopeless physical-medical condition,

Drowns and grinds you every day,

You strongly believe "If I can raise a child like Hrag, I can do anything,"

So, you move aggressively to expand your company's operations,

To conquer the universe in front of you.

Gradually, work-related recession issues,

Suppliers, vendors, and customers' daily headaches,

Declining profit margins, together with rising costs,

Make your corporate operations almost meaningless.

State, federal, and city tax reporting issues,

Paperwork requirements to run your operations,

That you have absolutely no energy to focus on and prepare,

Rising and uncollectible receivables, past due notices, late pay penalties, and cancellations

All hit you from every corner.

Hefty bi-monthly payrolls that come without sufficient funds to cover,

Workers comp frivolous and fabricated claims,

King-size capital obligations that you undertook,

In anticipation of substantial growth opportunities,

Have now turned upside down.

Depression is painted all over your face;

Your wife and children see it,

Your employees, vendors, and customers see it.

You just do not know where to start?

Which one to do first?

While the weight of your burden gets heavier and bigger every day.

This cannot be you, you think.

Someone who rose from almost nothing,

An immigrant student in a foreign land, with no family connections.

Someone with your educational and business background and experience,

Would not be in this kind of a quagmire.

A young bank executive, who in the late seventies,

Earned more than the California governor,

A financial expert analyst, who counseled major international corporate executives

How to efficiently run their operations,

Cannot be this mentally paralyzed and uncertain what to do.

From your childhood,

You have been the rock for so many families and organizations,

You always were a winner.

You never learned or tasted the meaning of losing in life.

Then you watch ex-governor John Connally of Texas,

The one who accompanied President Kennedy when he was assassinated,

Become treasury secretary of the U S,

You see his signature on all newly printed dollar currencies,

Then you watch him in a hotel conference room,

While they are auctioning his furniture and estate belongings in a bankruptcy filing,

Facing his problems head-on.

How did that happen to the treasury secretary of the U S?

He was entrusted with the treasury of the richest country in the world,

But he failed in his own family's finances.

Such a humble learning experience,

The best learning experience.

At least, the Lord saved me from hitting the real bottom.

I learned my lessons and was saved before I hit the bottom,

The Lord inspired my pianist wife to come to my rescue,

With no knowledge of business administration or how to run a company,

She came and took the lead of firing five of my top corporate executives,

She learned computerized order processing, customer service operations,

And monitoring accounts receivables, payables, and inventory controls,

She reduced my payroll enough to close the monthly drain,

And gave me time to stabilize my sinking ship.

When your arrogance gets shattered, you get humbled down to Earth where you should be,

Mine was the realization that I had no inherent value without the Lord,

Without Him in the center of my life, I can't do anything,

But with Him in me, I can do and achieve the impossible.

So, gradually you understand and analyze what happened and why.

With the full support of your wife and family

You start solving your problems one by one,

Day by day,

Step by step,

Until you get all your mental and emotional energy back.

And believe me,

You will overcome that depressing environment surrounding your mind and soul,

Your mind will be clear,

And your same mind will now soar to higher grounds than ever before.

If you have a deep rooted faith and trust in God,

In time,

You will conquer your depression.

SECTION II

PEARLS OF FAITH

SUNDAY MORNING

It is Sunday morning again,

It is time to reinvigorate and re energize

We are gathered as a church body in the House of our Lord,

To worship Him,

To praise His Almighty name,

To listen to His Holy words and yearning in our hearts.

We are gathered to renew and revitalize our minds and soul,

To be comforted by His immeasurable love,

To be strengthened and consoled by His peace.

We are gathered to turn a new page in our lives,

We are gathered to seek His wisdom and guidance,

To the many stressful, tough and difficult situations

We find ourselves in.

Lord, we messed up,

We desperately need help.

We are here to surrender the steering wheel of our lives to You.

Guide us, lead us to wherever and whatever you want us to do.

Lord, fill us with Your courage and belief,

That as long as You are with us,

We have absolutely nothing to worry about.

Let Thy will, be done.

GODLY HARMONY

I cherish harmony; it is a lifelong pursuit of mine.

I seek harmony in all my relationships,

Our mind functions at its best in harmonious environments and circumstances.

But, look around; do you see harmony?

Do you feel harmonious when you wake up?

I get scared to turn the television on or surf the internet, or read the daily newspaper,

Harmony has been chased out of our immediate surroundings,

Chaos and mayhem rule,

Riots spread in so many cities,

Perceived or real injustice happens every day.

Planned daily outbursts of new disorderly conduct,

Starts fire in so many locations that even breathing becomes difficult.

Violence for the sake of violence,

The rule of the jungle, where sheer physical power,

To intimidate, subjugate, and rule by ugly force,

Are useful tools and acceptable norms.

In the end, and believe me, this will end,

This chaos cannot and will not survive.

Harmony will come

Because harmony is Godly,

And GOD WILL WIN.

A NEW YEAR

Today is the beginning of a new year.

Hours ago, 2011 became history,

The dawning of 2012 just began,

The earth rotated upon its axis 365 times,

And made a complete circle around the sun.

This tiny earth, with its eight billion inhabitants,

Together with billions of other planets, stars, and moons,

Continued rotating and spinning around the center of the whole universe.

Our Creator,

Our Lord,

We all see and feel different times, months, and seasons as we rotate in space,

But God, in the center, is fixed.

HE IS THE ONLY PERMANENT THING IN LIFE.

Time was the same for Him millions of years ago,

Today, tomorrow, and for eternity,

HE IS THE FOCAL POINT OF LIFE.

As 2012 starts,

I wish we all take time and ponder in gratitude,

All that our Lord has bestowed upon us,

He is Father to each one of us,

He loves us unconditionally no matter how many careless things we do,

Let us all remember that,

Everyday we live is a gift from Him,

As we see our children and grandchildren grow,

Let us make sure to teach them

That, the fear of the Lord, the Love of our Lord,

Is the beginning of wisdom.

Let the Lord's love and peace flow abundantly in each one of our lives,

During all of 2012 and beyond.

YOU LIVE

Lord, you know that

None of us ever

Has had the honor of seeing You in person.

None of us ever

Has had the glory of touching Your sacred hands.

None of us ever

Has had the eternal joy of hearing Your voice.

None of us ever

Has had the tantalizing scent of Your presence.

None of us ever

Can show You to others as proof for our belief.

Yet, You live within us,

Your holy spirit embodies our appearance.

You touch us, when we read about Your glorious works.

You give us joy, when we hear about Your numerous miracles.

You console us, when we are lost in deep and painful depression.

You shine through us, when we witness and glorify Your Holy
name,

You are an eternal fountain of life, my Lord,

And You live,

Within the hearts and minds,

Of every living creature.

HE IS RISEN

Because He is risen,

I have an everlasting life.

Because He is risen,

I have everlasting hope.

Because He is risen,

I have everlasting love.

Because He is risen,

I have everlasting peace.

Because He is risen,

His holy spirit is eager to live

Within you and me

As living proof,

That He, is alive.

LEAD ME

Another year has passed,

So many people that I know

Are not with us anymore.

Yet I am going strong in good health,

Full of energy, vigor, and hope, with many new goals to achieve.

I believe that my best years are still ahead of me.

I am so happy and thankful that, to a great extent,

I have entrusted the steering wheel of my life

In the hands of our Creator, our Lord.

I have put my trust in Him.

I have stopped worrying about various challenges and bothersome
issues,

So many small and big problems,

Because He knows all of them, and they are all peanuts for Him.

So, thank you, Lord,

Lead me,

To wherever you want me to go,

I will follow and do whatever you want me to do.

Learn and trust how to do this with all your heart,

And in due course, see all your problems, big and small, disappear.

IT ALL GETS SO MURKY

In the midst of this Coronavirus epidemic, what do you think will happen?

How would you and your family be impacted by this international madness?

How many people will die?

How negatively will this impact your health and well-being?

How will it impact your job and finances?

How will it impact the city, state, or country we live in?

What do we have to do to remain safe and healthy?

How safe is it to go out and visit our family members, friends, and relatives?

Who do you listen to?

Where did this come from?

Who can get rid of this deadly virus?

It all is so murky right now.

We don't know what to do, how it happened, or who it will affect

For me, I am very calm and confident.

I have faced numerous uncertainties before;

Deep in my heart, I know this too shall pass,

The Lord always provides me a comforting shelter.

I AM ABSOLUTELY NOT AFRAID.

As a matter of fact,

I am confident that 2020 will be one of my best years ever.

IN GOD, I TRUST.

WE COME TO YOU

O lord,

Our heavenly Father,

Creator of the whole universe.

We come to You with heavy hearts and minds,

We come to You in severe pain,

We come to You with broken spirits,

We come to You with multiple ailments,

We come to You with hurt feelings and anger,

We come to You with mental and emotional despair,

We come to You subdued and humiliated,

We come to You defeated and humbled,

We come to You with all of our sins,

We come to You with all of our misfortunes,

We come to You with all of our temptations,

We come to You with all of our mischievous thoughts,

We come to You with all of our physical sicknesses,

We come to You with all of our family problems,

We come to You with all of our life-threatening emergencies,

We come to You exhausted and drained.

Yes, Lord, we come to You.

Through Your Son, Jesus Christ.

We have nowhere else to go.

You are our only hope and salvation.

Put our broken pieces and families together again.

We come to be healed,

We come to be nourished,

We come to be energized with faith,

We come to be brightened with hope and joy of life,

We come to glorify Your name.

We come to praise Your miracles and witness that

You can save us from any situation.

You are, God almighty,

You are the central meaning of life as we know it,

You created all,

And today, You live.

DO YOU HAVE A COMPASS?

Who is right?

Who is wrong?

Which one is the right path?

How can we find the truth?

How can we comprehend and make the right decision?

From the avalanche of misinformation we all face every day,

Life is murky, confusing, and complicated,

It is all planned to be that way.

So that at one point, we realize,

That we need a compass

To guide us through this mess,

To give direction and clarity to where we are heading.

We need the Lord in our heart, mind, and soul,

To show us how to make the right choices in our lives,

From the many alternatives, we all face every day.

May the Lord bring peace to your heart,

So that you believe that He is in control.

Let Him be your guide,

Your compass,

So that you know for sure where you are heading.

COUNT YOUR BLESSINGS

It is human nature to complain,

To focus on our real or perceived misfortunes:

The difficult circumstances we are in,

The financial stress and obligations we are burdened with,

And health-related deficiencies we live with.

We complain about the unfairness of it all.

We complain about the way we look.

Why don't I look like a movie star? We moan,

We complain about our health,

Improper hearing, weak eyesight,

Muscle ache, joint ache, backache,

We complain about snoring, high cholesterol.

We complain about the constant lack of financial resources.

Why did the lord give abundantly to our friends and relatives,

With so little to me?

It just does not seem fair, we think,

Hence, the mental anguish gives us

Greater reason to complain.

These are just a few;

We all have our own personal list of complaints.

Now, close your eyes for a moment,

Get rid of all negative thoughts from your mind.

Open your eyes,

Start counting the blessings that the Lord has given you.

Listen to your heart. It beats, yeah?

Well, thank God.

Thousands of hearts stopped beating

While you were reading this page.

Do you see your hands and feet?

All your fingers and toes are there, and you can move them.

Be thankful,

You can walk, talk, hear, see, feel, love, remember.

Be thankful,

Millions of people cannot do one or several of these.

If you do not like some of the circumstances you are in,

Either accept them or change them, if you can.

I know it might look impossible at first,

But a gradual change should give you enough hope.

Complaints get you nowhere.

Count your blessings, and be thankful for what you have.

There are millions of people in the Middle East, Africa, and Asia,

Who would do anything to trade places with you.

Yes, you.

So, start counting the blessings

The Lord has bestowed upon you;

Be happy and thankful

You indeed are better off,

Than millions of human souls

Just like you.

WHY AND HOW

As we navigate through life,

Many things happen to us and around us.

We go through various experiences;

We witness painful and horrific events

That our human brain can not comprehend and analyze.

From our childhood, our Christian faith has taught us that

God is just,

He is fair

He is everywhere,

He knows all things present and future,

He created and controlled the whole universe,

And nothing happens without His awareness

He has good plans for all of us,

We also know that He created us like His image,

Gave us authority over all His creations,

With our firm beliefs and knowledge,

Our human brain starts to wonder,

About all the inconsistencies, injustice, and illogical events,

We see all around us throughout the years.

Why did our Lord create us imperfect? We wonder.

We all have imperfections,

Some very apparent,

While others we hide from the outside world

Why?

Why aren't we physically, emotionally, and mentally perfect?

It almost feels like our physical and emotional entities have
missing parts,

Or a malfunctioning device,

Requiring occasional fixing, monitoring, and fine-tuning,

Without which we could easily fall apart,

Why?

We all have big egos,

We always look for me, mine, and our interests

Why?

Why is it that we are never satisfied?

Whatever physical things we like or enjoy, we always want more
and more,

Why do we habitually lie, cheat, and misbehave?

Many times without realizing that we do,

Because it has become second nature.

Why do we lust?

If it's sinful to do so,

If it's sinful to fantasize about spending time with a special
opposite sex,

Which keeps haunting us during our resting time,

Why didn't our Lord remove that particular gene from our brain?

We all know the difference between right and wrong,

Legal and illegal,

Moral and immoral,

Decent and indecent,

But many times, we face temptations and make wrong choices.

Why?

If you seriously look at our civilization throughout history,

You see so many instances of inequality and injustice.

Why?

Why would God allow so many religions, offshoots, and sects to flourish?

Why would God allow so many wars to occur?

Why are so many babies killed through abortion?

Why do bad things happen to a lot of good people?

Why are so many corrupt and inept individuals, are elevated to positions of power and rule,

Why is it that few people are allowed to be very successful and rich,

While millions live with severe depravity,

Why do we have hunger and starvation?

Why do we have ongoing wars,

If billions of stars and planets rotate in God's universe in perfect harmony?

Why do we have so much disharmony amongst nations?

How could our Omnipotent Creator be so blind to injustice?

Why would He allow evil to even exist?

Or allow evil-doers to keep winning and having the upper hand.

How could the Prince of Peace allow so much savagery and inhumanity?

How could our Omnipresent Lord not interfere, help, heal and protect His flock?

From natural disasters, earthquakes, tornados, hurricanes, tsunamis, and volcanoes,

How could He not see our painful tears or hear our heartfelt prayers?

These are just a few of my 'why' and 'how' painful inquiries,

I am sure you have your own lengthy questions in your mind, tormenting you for years,

Unanswered and will remain so for the rest of your life,

For that is the basis of our faith,

We have to live our lives trusting our God

He is the only perfect one,

He is God,

He owes no explanation to any of us,

He is the Creator, we the created.

All our surroundings are a gift,

He can take it away, whenever He chooses.

We should not torment our minds in order to understand God's
motive or purpose,

We will never know or comprehend what He knows

Or see what He sees,

The only 'why' and 'how' we have to worry about,

How?

How soon can we find His son, Jesus Christ?

Who came to this world and shed His Godly blood for us,

How soon can we feel His presence in our minds and soul?

Why?

So that we can have eternal life,

So that we can live in peace and harmony in this world,

So that living with life's challenges, inconsistencies and turmoil,

Can be bearable and meaningful.

And finally,

So that we can see and feel that we are all his children,

He loves us,

He will take care of us,

And He will protect us and has good plans for us,

Just like we take care of our own children.

That's exactly why

I do not ask these questions anymore,

Because he loves me as I am.

POWER

Power corrupts our minds,

Power tarnishes our soul,

Power in the hands of a narcissist

Cannot co-exist with God's teachings,

Power hungry individuals

Will always justify their deeds.

They will always use their position of power

To fool, to convince, to rationalize, to lie,

To fabricate events and stories, to justify their narrative.

Power-hungry individuals will surround themselves,

With intellectually weak or unprepared team members,

So that no one can challenge his or her authority.

They always have to be the main event,

The main actor, the main brain and initiator,

THEY HAVE TO BE THE CENTRAL LIMELIGHT.

For them, keeping their position of power is vital;

The end justifies any means,

Complete fabrication of lies, unethical and illegal acts,

False witnesses, inappropriate rumors,

All are valid means to defeat an opposing person or opinion.

A hunger for absolute power erodes your faith in God,

A hunger for absolute power provides a cozy shelter to Satan.

Christ, as Son of God, had all the power given to Him,

All the power was in Him

Yet, against all injustice, all humiliation,

All physical and emotional abuse,

All temptations to use His power,

To punish the unfaithful, the unjust, and evildoers.

To show all who is King of Kings,

He never used His power,

"An eye for an eye" did not cross His mind,

Even when He was being nailed to the cross.

They hung and crucified Him,

He still cried,

"Lord forgive them, they do not know what they are doing."

Real men of faith do not abuse their power,

But rather use it to glorify God

Real men of faith fight for justice, peace, and spreading of God's love and grace,

Even at the expense of their own temporary demise.

Real men of God do not seek power;

Power comes to them on autopilot.

The best way to learn how to use real power

Is to learn it from Christ, the only Son of God,

THE ONE WHO HAS ALL THE POWER IN HIS HANDS.

WHY IS IT SO DIFFICULT?

Lord, why is it so difficult to serve you?

How can we continue serving you?

When there are so many who supposedly serve you with full compensation?

Who are clueless,

So many, who have no backbone,

Who have no understanding of Godly principles,

Who have no faith and courage to defend the truth,

But they do have positions of being your mouthpiece,

Their ego so prominently promoted in every occasion,

Lord, these worthless hypocrites,

In effect, make a mockery of your teachings,

They make it so difficult,

For real believing men and women,

To experience the presence of Your Holy Spirit,

The Divine humility that you exemplified,

With your own life's example,

Lord, cleanse and expunge these fake paid conveyors of your message,

Because they tarnish Your Holy name,

Their presence acts as a repellent for gathering of the faithful.

Some of these fraudulent sinisters,

Have penetrated your structural ranks,

With great skill,

They have mastered the art of operating in disguise in plain sight,

Prominently exhibiting their bogus pious façade.

All that easily works to fool the naive inattentive populace,

But, You, know everyone's heart and soul,

You know who they are by name,

In Your own proper time and will,

Cleanse and strengthen Your church as You see fit.

Coming from a concerned humble servant,

Who sees and can't be easily fooled,

Nor stay silent to this glaring hypocrisy

LIFE'S ROLLER COASTERS

When we have pristine weather,

Blue skies and unpolluted visibility,

It is easy to navigate.

Through our daily lives,

But obstacles arise,

Unexpected accidents occur,

Violent mental and emotional attack strike us left and right,

Our reservoir of ability, knowledge, and strength gets stretched thin,

To its maximum tolerance.

Can we keep this human ship afloat, we wonder?

These are our lives' critical tests.

Do we succumb under the weight?

Or, do we rise up against all our challenges,

With a victorious counter-attack.

Our Lord takes us through these roller coasters quite often,

If you have His company with you,

Nothing should scare you.

JUST KEEP CALM AND KEEP GOING,

Knowing full well that while He is in control,

You have nothing to worry about.

HE NEVER FAILS

We all have loved ones,

Who we know sometimes need non-financial help:

The kind of help that we usually

Can't do anything about it.

That is when we have to learn how to pray:

Pray for them by name,

And pray for the specific situation.

Put it on a silver platter, and place it on the altar of our Creator,

And watch the good Lord

Do what He does best.

Trust that your prayers will be answered, because

HE NEVER FAILS

PURIFICATION

Purifying our lives with Christ,

Is a lifelong commitment.

Purifying our lives,

To be like Christ,

Is again, a lifelong commitment.

Unattainable, yes.

Because only He

Is the son of God.

But we can gradually mold ourselves

To follow in His footsteps.

As long as you are in that steadfast pursuit,

Do not worry,

He will do the rest.

AND LEAD US NOT INTO TEMPTATION

The importance of these words from the Lord's Prayer,

Mathew 6: 9 to 13 comes to my mind quite often.

Wondering why? The Son of God felt,

It should be included in the Lord's Prayer.

He left out so many other important subjects to include in the most important prayer,

But included "temptation,"

I am sure he knew the importance of this,

Because from the beginning,

Adam and Eve, God's first human creation,

Were tempted and failed.

We all get tempted quite often, almost daily,

When you come face to face with it,

How is your willpower to fight temptation?

Do you have enough strength, determination, and knowledge that

Nothing good will come out of temptation.

Avoid it at all costs,

Disconnect yourself from whoever is leading you to temptation,

And find inner joy and peace.

TIME WITH YOU

I have a strong yearning,

To spend time with you,

O Lord,

A time to reflect,

A time to feel at home,

A time to comfort,

A time to re-energize,

A time to be so thankful,

For all the time you have given to me,

A time to pray,

About all the challenges I face,

A time to renew my trust and belief,

That you know all that is going on with my life,

You know all my inner thoughts,

And at the proper time,

All will be good.

Time with you, o Lord,

Is the most rewarding time I can ever have.

A PRAYER OF VICTORY

You, my Lord, bestowed onto me,

Numerous and plentiful gifts of beauty and value,

A rather comfortable standard of living all throughout,

You gave me a high education, wisdom, and wealth,

Ranking positions in various institutions,

You gave me a wife, who completely entices my mind,

You gave me three children, who enrich my life,

You gave me financial capability,

That allowed me to own or enjoy whatever my heart and mind
desired,

I, my Lord, had the audacity to think,

That I was responsible for all these gifts,

I deserved it,

I earned it,

I built it,

And, I am the rightful title holder of all.

Now, my Lord,

Knelt and in tears, accept my broken self,

My broken ego,

Without you, my Lord,

I AM NOTHING.

NOTHING.

You are the reason for my life,

You are the meaning of my life,

You are the center of my life.

Forgive me, my Lord,

Forgive me from the biggest of sins.

Cleanse me from my ego,

Let my ego be crushed in front of your Almighty name,

Since you are the Life and the Truth.

Without You, my Lord, I am nothing.

But with your Grace and permission,

Transform me into a radiant morning sunrise.

To glow and shine Your everlasting Truth and Love.

With crystal tears of joy and thankfulness.

EMPTINESS IS WHERE SATAN REIGNS

Sometimes, life shows its ugly emptiness.

Everything turns dull and muted,

With all energies and desires sucked out of you.

Solitude becomes your best friend,

You are unappreciated, unloved, misunderstood by those close to

you.

You are surrounded with egocentric, jealous souls.

You question why you tolerated them for so long,

You gaze inward in your deeper mind and soul,

And search the vastness of the sky,

For some meaning, for some light,

That all this could not have been a complete waste,

It could not have been all in vain,

The emptiness surrounding our lives can't be Satan's reign,

There must be beauty,

There must be life,

There must be music,

There must be a new sunrise,

Beyond every depressed, empty soul,

There must be God's creation of you and me,

THE LOVE OF LIFE ITSELF, TO SEE, TO FEEL AND THEN

SHARE.

BABY JESUS

God created the whole universe in seven days,

But all His creations

Became meaningful by the birth of baby Jesus,

The only Son of God.

The Lord realized that

Something was missing

In the world He created.

Love was missing,

Peace was missing,

Forgiveness was missing,

Hope was missing,

Faith in God Almighty was missing,

The promise of eternal life was missing,

So, He decided to send His only Son,

Baby Jesus,

As the culmination of His creation,

As the salvation of what He created,

So that all who believe, feel, and see,

Find the real meaning of life.

Find out why they were born.

Find out why they were created.

A SIMPLE PRAYER

Lord,

At some point in the future

I will not be around,

Like billions of people before me,

I will also faithfully depart

After I am gone,

Help me to be remembered,

As a good father, husband, and grandfather,

Three most important and interconnected aspects of life,

The essence of who we are.

Please guide me to be a better,

Husband, father, and grandfather,

Through whatever days and years are still left in me,

All other things and duties are secondary.

A simple path and prayer,

If we all follow,

And teach our children to do the same,

Our world will be a better place to live.

PURPOSEFUL LIVING

We are born as precious babies some years ago,

We start moving, laughing, crying, crawling

And finally, talking,

Bringing heavenly joy to our parents.

As we start walking and grasping our surroundings,

Our parents send us to preschool, kindergarten, and high school;

We grow up reading, studying, learning,

And accumulating all kinds of information and knowledge.

We start forming a personality, a character, a belief system,

If we were good in school,

We would continue on to college and university,

To specialize in a field we've developed an interest in.

Upon graduation, we find employment in a field,

We feel a bright future is stored for us,

Once our employment is secure,

We look for a soulmate, a wife, a husband,

To share life's challenges, happiness, and joy together,

Hopefully, God will bless us with children,

One, two, three, or however many the Lord provides,

During which we participate in a divine task of

Creating another human being.

A child of God.

As your children go through the same process you went through,

You feel obligated to provide for your children

Things that were not provided to you.

Clothing, medical expenses, education tuition, housing,

Automobile expenses, insurance expenses, and food on the table

Force you to put in long hours at work.

You might ask your spouse to work also to lighten your load,

You both work harder and harder to receive good things in life,

And pay the never-ending mortgage payments,

Credit card payments,

Lease payments,

Medical payments,

Tax payments,

Commuting back and forth on the freeway in constant traffic,

And bumper-to-bumper rides ruin your nerves and physique.

Your kids grow up and get involved

In all sorts of misbehavior,

All your guidance, prayers, schooling, and love for them,

Seems to have been wasted.

Life shows its ugly sides in so many ways.

You might suffer a job loss, unemployment, serious illness,

Divorce, emotional distress.

And as you speed through life to meet every commitment,

Every obligation and task.

Suddenly you realize that you are in your fifties,

And you start questioning and asking yourself,

Where did I go wrong?

Am I on the right path?

Has it all been worth it?

Where am I going?

Have I left my positive and lasting footprint in life?

If I leave today, what would they say about me?

How would my family, friends, and relatives remember me?

Did I serve any purpose in life besides satisfying my own needs?

Has it been all about me, and my education?

My marriage, my family, my business?

And finally, why am I living? What for?

Questions and questions

Bothersome but worthwhile questions.

I hope and pray that

As we travel through life,

We find time to realize and understand that

Our life is a gift from God,

Lent to us for a short period of time,

To find and enjoy God's love, harmony, and glory,

Not only for us and our family,

But to share, give, and distribute

God's abundant blessings and love with others,

Especially to people we've never met,

With no expectations in return

Only then our life will be full and rewarding,

Our life will be meaningful;

Because giving and sharing is a Godly art,

And will bring purpose to our lives.

LORD, WHERE ARE YOU?

Lord, your absence is so glaring.

Your presence is so needed in so many countries,

And your lack of attention to human suffering is unexplainable,

Millions and millions are praying their heart out every day,

They are being killed, beheaded, crucified, expelled, burned alive,

Bombed, turned homeless, and scared to death of what's to come.

Innocent young children are being traumatized and maimed for life,

Vengeance, hatred, and brutal barbarism are spreading like wildfire,

People commit so many atrocities by proclaiming "Allah hu Akbar";

What kind of a god are they talking about?

What kind of a god would condone all this hate, killing, and destruction?

Our daily media is turning poisonous,

Our daily air is getting difficult to breathe,

LORD, YOUR PRESENCE IS NEEDED,

YOUR LOVE IS NEEDED,

YOUR PEACE IS NEEDED,

YOU HAVE TO SHOW WHO IS KING OF KINGS,

So that all nations can stop this expanding, senseless orgy of hate and violence

Going on in so many countries, all at the same time.

YOU CANNOT ALLOW EVIL TO REIGN IN OUR WORLD.

July 2014

DAILY PRAYER

Being in daily communication with the Lord

Puts my mind at ease and at peace.

I do the best I can,

The tasks I have to do, or should do,

The things I can't do or things that are beyond my ability to
handle.

For the time being,

I leave it for the Lord to handle.

He has never disappointed me;

He keeps me emotionally dependent on Him,

Which is exactly where I want to be:

Dependent on Him.

Because

I simply do not know anyone

More dependable than the Lord. It is a prudent and steadfast
principle

For all to follow.

CREATED BY HIS IMAGE

When God created Adam,

He created him with His image.

His image referred to here,

I believe it is our brain:

Our mind.

That is where we can think,

That is where we can imagine, love, feel, plan, and soar,

With no limits whatsoever

And with no boundaries whatsoever.

So today,

Do you feel the power of this 'Image' in you?

Break your walls,

Shatter your ceiling,

The boundaries, restrictions, and self-imposed limits, and

Let your God-given mind

Fly, soar, and achieve,

Whatever you can imagine.

You are made in God's image,

There is no limit to what you can accomplish.

THE MISSING INGREDIENT

We have so much confusion and chaos in the world.

So many conflicting opinions, objectives, and goals

Between nations and nationalities,

Between races,

Between sexes,

Between families,

Between parents and their children,

Between husbands and wives,

And between the best of friends and lovers.

It is so difficult to establish

Who is right?

Who is wrong?

What is the truth?

Amongst all these conflicts and chaos,

We all forget to recognize and remember,

The glaring, main message of our Lord:

LOVE.

As the main remedy and cure of all conflict, confusion, chaos, and calamity,

LOVE indeed is the missing ingredient,

In all of our imperfect human relationships.

IT WOULD HAVE BEEN SO NICE

It would have been so nice,

If the Lord made our lives a little simpler.

Less things to do,

Less obligations to meet,

Less tangled relationships,

Less problems to solve,

Less traffic congestion to fight,

Less bills to pay,

Less emotional turmoil and strain in our daily lives,

Less deadlines to meet.

Actually, it would have been so niceIf we simply had everything
our heart and mind desired,

With no effort on our part,

I assume you all will agree that, yes,

That would have been so ideal.

But the reality is

That life is very complex,

Human relationships are complex,

Our physical body is complex,

Our needs and desires are intricate and contradictory,

Our goals in life are in constant change,

Our circle of friends and relatives is so diverse,

The daily information and news we are bombarded with

Are so confusing and manipulative,

And through it all,

If we just can see

That life,

God's creation,

Is just right,

Simple, but complex and incomprehensible:

Just the way it should be,

In perfect harmony.

I AM NOT A PERFECTIONIST

I do not have the desire to be a perfectionist,

If I get 85% to 90% of what I want,

I am very happy.

I did not have to be a perfectionist

To be the first in my class, all throughout high school.

Not achieving 100% of my goals,

Does not bother me either,

The pillows on the couch do not have to be

Exactly at a forty-five-degree angle,

A little slant of the picture frames hanging in the living room

Does not bother me that much.

It is okay if my shirt and tie sometimes do not match,

It is okay if people around me know some of my imperfections;

I do have a few.

I know the Lord created us with His image,

But we are always a copy.

He was and continues to be the only Original.

He never intended us to be perfect,

Just a copy,

Dependent on Him: THE ORIGINAL.

IF WITH ALL YOUR HEART

On Sunday,

My wife was playing the piano during church service,

"If with all your heart,

You truly seek me,

You will find me."

The music, the tune, and the words,

Gave me a deep desire to seek,

To seek the love and peace

That only Christ can provide.

Amen.

WILL HE EVER HAVE TIME FOR ME?

I am seeking an opportunity to have a one-on-one meeting with our

Creator.

Will He ever have time for me?

One human soul,

A tiny little sampling of His creation.

If He put the brainpower in me to imagine and ponder,

The immenseness of the universe we know,

The faraway, billions of galaxies still have yet to be discovered.

Will He ever have time for me?

In my heart, I know He does,

He is directing and orchestrating my path,

I am so confident that the Almighty

Is there, watching and guiding every step I take.

For that deep-seated knowledge and belief

I am eternally grateful.

He, is also watching and guiding you.

MIRROR-MIRROR ON THE WALL

When you look in the mirror?

Naturally, you see yourself.

When others look at you?

Who do you think they see?

Do you think they see the real you?

How accurate do you think their perception of who the real you is?

Because most people know each other superficially.

Usually, they only know what you let them know:

Partial glimpses of you, here and there.

One person, however, does not need a mirror to see you properly,

You will never impress Him with your outside looks or façade,

The Lord knows who you are,

He knows you inside out.

He is the most important Person you have to impress.

Sometimes, we work for a whole lifetime to portray a certain image of ourselves,

Our looks, clothing, profession, education, position,

So that we can impress whoever is looking at us.

In the end, we have to come to realize,

We will be completely naked in front of our Creator,

With all our life's scars fully exposed.

Mirror, mirror, what would the Lord be looking at?

THE PRESENCE OF THE HOLY SPIRIT

It takes a lot of mental effort and concentration

To feel the presence of the Holy Spirit in our lives,

There is so much systemic pollution and impurities all around us,

Blocking the communion of the Holy Spirit,

With our inner soul and mind.

The Holy Spirit is living and floating all around us,

Waiting for us to feel and acknowledge His presence,

Feel His love,

Feel His peace,

Feel His comfort and harmony, and

Absorb the purification of our mind and heart.

May we all have an opportunity to experience the thrill,

The mental-spiritual sight,

To see, feel, and cherish,

The eternal joy of the presence of the Holy Spirit,

All around our lives,

Knowing full well

That our destiny is firmly in His hand,

We do not have to worry.

CAN'T SLEEP AT NIGHT

If you can't sleep properly at night?

I have a simple cure for you that works well for me, quite often.

Even though once I put my head on my pillow,

I usually fall asleep within a few minutes.

But yesterday for some reason, it took longer,

So, I kick my process of praying.

First was a prayer of thanks for all that God has bestowed upon
me,

Then, one by one, I went through my family members:

My wife, children, grandchildren, relatives, friends, church
members

And so on.

I prayed by each person's name and the special needs that I knew
they had.

By the time I got to the last number that I do not remember,

I was already asleep.

Try it; it works.

I do not know a better way to fall asleep.

Later on, monitor the results of your prayers,

And witness the answer to your prayers the Lord provides.

Have a good night's sleep.

WHAT'S MY NEXT MOVE?

I do the best I can today,

Diligently planning what I should do next,

Six months, twelve months forward and beyond.

Somehow I feel the Lord is putting me

In front of individuals, circumstances, and situations

That are opening new windows and doors

To the next stages of my life.

So I stopped questioning how it happened.

I did not pursue this. I did not plan this.

How did it appear on my path?

I feel like the Master Chess Player

Has full control of my life's chessboard,

Playing my life's chess game

One move at a time.

With the full knowledge that

As long as He is in charge of my life's chessboard,

Occasionally He has to sacrifice a pawn or a bishop,

To eventually achieve eternal victory.

BEING REBORN

The question I have with being reborn

And the question I have with spiritual birth is,

Who determines one is reborn?

How do you measure that you are maturing in your walk with Christ?

There are so many who call themselves being reborn,

Yet bring shame and disgrace to the ultimate prize of life.

Does simply stating one is reborn

Make it so?

Who verifies?

Who certifies?

That yes, indeed, such and such person is reborn.

Being reborn is a transformation of our life:

Transformation of the way we act,

Transformation of the way we react,

Transformation of the way we live,

Transformation of the way we talk,

Transformation of the way we love, forgive, and share

All of God's blessings with others.

If you feel and know you are reborn,

Make sure the way you talk and the way you act

Are in sync and reflect that you indeed are reborn.

DO NOT DEPRIVE YOURSELF

During yesterday's church service, two things resonated with me:

First, from the sermon, the pastor mentioned how Thomas Edison

Failed over 1,000 times

Before he invented the light bulb.

Secondly, a verse from one of the hymns we sang:

"On Christ, the solid rock I stand,

All other ground is sinking sand."

Friend, if you are not going to the house of your Lord on a regular

basis,

YOU ARE LOSING OUT.

The sooner you realize that, the better.

Our mind, heart, and soul need nourishment,

Just like our body needs food, so

DO NOT DEPRIVE YOURSELF.

INNER NEEDS

Whatever your inner needs are,

I hope today will be the day.

God will give you an answer.

His timing is perfect;

Expect it to happen.

SPRINGTIME

I love springtime,

Especially in the San Gabriel mountains of California,

When multicolored roses bloom,

When the fruit trees start producing their respective fruits,

When the weather becomes so inviting

When the birds come and sing to me in my backyard,

Telling me about things I don't understand,

When the mild wind whispers softly through the valley,

When the wild cactus shows its magnificent vibrancy,

When the lush greenery covers the surrounding mountain range,

When the San Gabriel river runs aimlessly down its rocky bed,

When God declares from the blue skies above,

"This is all for you,

Absorb it,

Breathe it all in,

Digest it and enjoy it."

To Him be the glory.

MY BACKYARD

What a joy to sit and have my morning coffee in my backyard,

Enjoying God's majesty and creation,

The green mountain ranges surrounding me,

The blooming flowers all around,

The relaxing sound of the waterfall in the fishpond and pool,

The uninvited, but always welcomed, variety of San Gabriel
mountain birds,

Singing and chirping their hearts out in coordinated, orchestral
harmony,

While another jaybird was feeding four of its newborns underneath
my balcony,

Yet, bigger falcons high in the sky flip and fly up north.

I watch and listen to this natural wonder being played for me live,

Crafted for me on the spot.

I sip my coffee,

Absorbing the inner beauty of this scene and the natural harmony all around,

And I say, *Thank you, Lord.*

SECTION III

PEARLS OF

PATRIOTISM

I AM PROUD TO BE AN AMERICAN

I am proud to be an American,

For this is the country of the free,

This is the country where people and its government trust in God,

This is the country where people express their thoughts with little fear,

This is the country where people worship who they please,

This is a country built on its people of unimaginable backgrounds,

People from various races, religions, nationalities, and wealth,

Living and working together in relative harmony,

And bound together with a common goal,

To preserve "the American way."

Since this country is the best there is,

And I say that with no prejudice,

Not because I was born here,

Because I wasn't.

I say it because I've lived in other countries,

I have been in over thirty of them,

And every time I left the American shores,

I counted the days remaining for my return.

While overseas, I always miss our clean streets,

Our manicured and green lawns,

Our purified waters and blue skies,

Our reasonably priced groceries and restaurants

And the availability of everything your heart desires.

Yes, this is my country.

I love it with all my heart

And I am ready to defend it with all I have in me,

Let no zealot misjudge the American spirit.

And why do I love America?

I love it for its fair laws;

All are treated equally, from president to janitor.

All have a clear pathway to get educated and succeed.

People govern themselves through democratically elected individuals.

We have one of the fairest tax systems,

We take care of our poor,

We take care of our elderly,

We take care of the weak and the unemployed,

We help financially and morally almost every country in this world,

We help rebuild the countries of our friends,

We help rebuild the countries of our enemies or ex-enemies,

We do not conquer other lands,

But we like to trade and prosper,

So that all can benefit,

Yes, I know, we have our faults and sins,

We make mistakes, but we learn and change our ways.

I am an American citizen,

Yes, I am of Armenian origin,

But America is my land,

America is the country I am ready to die for.

Ara and Esther,
With best wishes and appreciation,

WORRY BEADS

Tomorrow is President Biden's inauguration day,

I worry about all of the irregularities during his election,

I worry about all of the social media manipulations we went
through,

I worry about all the restrictions being imposed on us,

I worry about the gradually shrinking freedoms we enjoy in the
U.S.

I worry about COVID-19 and the continuously increasing death
toll.

I worry about the vaccine itself that is supposed to halt the spread
of this pandemic.I worry about all these irrational shutdowns and
their impact on millions of people.

I worry about where we are heading,

When the government keeps spending money,

But restricts the creation of revenue sources to pay for it.

I worry because it does not take rocket science to see

That we are being pushed towards a major economic cliff.

Throughout the years, I have accumulated a variety of worry beads;

Some were given to me as gifts,

Some I purchased to mentally reinforce and continue practicing.

What I have seen all around me as I was growing up,

Elderly individuals playing with their beads,

Moving the beads one by one with their thumb

As a natural habit to release mental anxiety.

Just keep pushing the beads.

Funny, I guess, I am in that age group now,

And I have to start using those worry beads.

Until now, I have used them as decorations in my office;

All of my worries are now at my fingertips.

I just push them away, one at a time.

Life will go on, I guess.

THE LAND OF THE FREE

Over fifty years ago,

I came to the United States.

Primarily to study finance and International business management,

And also because

For centuries, America was THE LAND OF THE FREE.

We sure do not hear about that anymore.

As a matter of fact, one by one,

Our freedoms have been curtailed and boxed in small cubicles.

This land of the free has turned into a mockery.

The new accepted practice is

Social distancing, an abhorrent fabrication.

Quarantine yourself at home,

And put on a mask when you leave your house for dire necessities.

This Coronavirus has paralyzed our minds,

With our own will, we are limiting our freedom,

To go to work,

To go to school,

To go to church,

Or to wherever we want to go.

Tell me, please, calm my skepticism;

Who knows the exact number of deaths

Caused solely by COVID-19?

I can assure you that the answer is dramatically lower than the announced count,

Being given to us hourly and daily to immobilize our minds.

If you give a substantial financial incentive

To hospitals and mortuaries, to certify deaths by COVID-19,

Naturally, that is what they will do.

Even though the person who died had multiple ailments,

There are no financial rewards for deaths by other ailments.

So, you call it death by Coronavirus

And pocket the money.

The state uses the growing count to justify,

Putting severe restrictions on our freedom.

I, for one, am not buying this charade;

I have no problem with fighting and finding a cure for this virus,

But do not restrict my freedom.

That is very un-American,

I detest wearing a mask,

And breathing in my own carbon dioxide,

How is that supposed to help?

It's unhealthy.

I am not in a herd;

I can not follow the rules and regulations that make no sense to me.

I cherish my freedom

As long as I am not hurting anyone.

I can not allow anyone to limit my freedom,

And what no foreign enemy has dared to do,

We did it to ourselves,

With our own hands,

And with our own cowardly submission.

We let the sick minds of unelected medical professionals

Shut down the US economy

And cause worldwide economic devastation,

All orchestrated and rationalized by inept leaders.

Mentally, I am an American economic soldier;

Working is my battlefield.

Working, producing, and safeguarding

A prosperous future for my grandchildren.

This oxygenates my blood,

That's what I will do.

If I have to die,

I would rather die while on duty, on the battlefield,

Like real men do.

The thought of leaving this world,

Cowardly imprisoning myself at home,

Makes me sick.

Even though my home indeed is a paradise for me,

And I love and enjoy staying home with my wife.

But when you restrict my movement out at my own will,

Then, my home becomes my own prison, which I abhor.

We have done enough damage,

Enough is enough.

Let's go back to work,

Quarantine the medical doctors to their hospitals,

Let them stay there until they find a cure for this virus,

So that we can enjoy this land,

This land of the free

May 2020.

THE REAL PICTURE

It is so difficult to see the real picture:

The real story,

The real facts.

Look here,

No, no, no, look there.

Have you heard about this?

Don't believe what they say;

They are all lies. Who is paying who?

To create and fabricate "facts."

Which ones are fake?

Which ones are real?

Who is behind all this commotion and confusion?

Who is behind all this misinformation and manipulation?

Leave me alone.

At this point,

I don't give a damn.

Don't you realize

That's how you rule and manage a crowd,

That's how you operate in a modern democracy,

Confuse them,

Scare them,

Make them feel very uncomfortable and vulnerable,

Make them realize the complexity of the crisis they are all in,

Then, show them the light.

Give them the solution, their salvation,

It doesn't matter if it's the right solution,

It doesn't matter if it's right or wrong,

Just kick the ball forward,

Make it disappear,

Maybe

Just maybe, the ball will dissolve by itself.

By then, you won't be there anyway,

For now, focus on

WINNING.

July 2020

ARE WE ON THE RIGHT PATH?

December 1991 is etched in my brain,

As the year the Soviet Union collapsed.

Since then, I've always wondered about

The mental anguish of millions of people in the fifteen Soviet
republics.

That's a total of 262 million people,

Who for seventy-four years

Followed a political, economic, and social system

They believed in fervently.

They gave their lives for it,

They defended it with all their strength,

But suddenly, the whole system collapsed and disintegrated.

The whole union of fifteen republics shattered,

All of the ideological, political, economic theories

Were proven to be wrong and flawed,

Outdated and unproductive for human development.

As people living within that system,

How would you mentally process what happened?

And the fact that you, your parents and grandparents,

Were on the wrong road all this time,

When all the things you have been taught at school,

Or read in newspapers, magazines, and books,

Now have turned out to be fabricated, false, or misrepresented.

With your present poor living conditions as proof of that failure,

How would you now function or believe?

That what you are reading, seeing, or hearing is true or fabricated,

For three generations, you have been blindly on the wrong path,

Many times by force,

How would you know you are on the right path now?

How much of what happened within the Soviet Union,

Is it happening in the West and the US?

Are we really immune from mass indoctrination and manipulation?

You bet we are not;

History repeats itself. If it worked that long on millions of people
for three generations

It will work easier and much better now,

Because we are so intricately socially connected and vulnerable,

False facts and situations easily convert themselves

To truths and ugly, unacceptable realities.

Are we on the right path, I wonder?

MR PRESIDENT,

US CONGRESS,

PRESIDENTIAL CANDIDATES:

DO YOU HAVE ANY IDEA WHERE AMERICA IS HEADING?

June 2008

Where we have come to, is simply a result of cumulative decisions, or lack of them that our government leaders have taken in the past decade. I know some outcomes and results are unpredictable because there are just too many variables to consider; however, in many cases, based on proven economic and scientific theories, it's quite easy to predict the future effects of our present decisions.

How did we get into this mess? And how do we get ourselves out of it? We all want our political leaders to navigate the world's biggest economy out of its present-day misery.

ENERGY POLICY, OR LACK OF ONE.

We believe in a free market. Naturally, the present thinking basically lets free market conditions develop and dictate energy policy. However, free markets have a very short-term horizon. If there are no payback within one, two, or three years, nothing will be done.

Developing energy resources takes a much longer life span. Accordingly, the government's direction and leadership is needed to develop energy resources, where investment payback could take ten to twenty years.

No matter how you look at it, energy production, in all its forms—gas, coal, nuclear, solar, natural gas, electric, wind, battery—is a major component of the U.S. economy. At the moment, we have a mismatch between oil supply and demand, i.e., the demand outpaces the available supply on a worldwide basis, leading to higher prices. However, why do we have a mismatch? How come we did not predict this way in advance? Why didn't we take appropriate action to remedy this mismatch? This imbalance did not happen in one day, one month, or one year. It's a gradual process with adequate time to shift to alternative energy resources.

At what point do we wake up and say enough is enough? We can not take this anymore. We have the brightest minds in the world with unmatched financial resources. If we do not lead, who will?

We have a federal reserve system handling our monetary policy. Who is handling our energy policy? The heads of central banks from the group of seven industrialized nations meet annually to coordinate their financial policies. Why don't we have a body like that, composed of major energy users, to coordinate and agree on an international energy policy? Who are we waiting for? Do we wait until a barrel of oil is $400.00 before we wake up? If we allow this trend to continue at the same rate as the past year, we will be there by the end of 2009-10. Then what?

If we have current technology to double or triple gas mileage/gallon in cars, then why aren't we pushing a lot harder to make cars that drive fifty miles/gallon or one hundred miles / gallon vs the twenty to twenty-five miles per gallon average now?

How could any commodity be allowed to increase 480% since 2001? When U.S. oil consumption grew roughly 17% for the same period? An inquiring mind would like to know.

Oil was at $28.00/barrel when we were hit on 9-11. At seventeen million barrels per day consumption during 2001, there are 6.2 billion barrels/year. Times $28.00 this costs us $178 billion/year. At $135.00/barrel and twenty million barrels/day consumption now, we are spending $985 billion/year. What a spectacular siphoning of national wealth.

I can bet my life that the price of oil will start dropping substantially if the president, in consultation with the U.S. Congress, delivers a thoughtful speech about America's firm commitment to forcefully develop alternative energy resources and immediately take the necessary political and economic measures in that pursuit, including tax incentives, to make certain alternative energy resources become more attractive.

Visiting Saudi Arabia and asking them to pump 300,000 barrels of more oil per day at these high prices will only make the Saudis richer and America poorer. Having a major international energy users forum about reducing oil usage to levels substantially below the current worldwide production of eighty-five million barrels per day, increasing the efficiency of our energy resources, and developing alternative energy supplies will eventually stop this upward spiraling madness and lower gas prices.

It's time to wake up. We have to lead, not led to the poor house. We have to attack our energy crisis from various areas. Which alternative energy resource is best for us is subject to discussion and scientific evaluation? but we do have choices, and we have to make them soon.

IRAQ WAR. PLUGGING THE ECONOMIC DRAIN

I have voted for President Bush twice, and I still think he is an honorable human being. For a long time, my position on the war was that the Commander in Chief knows more than I do, and he has more confidential information than the general public; accordingly, following our president's leadership was a sensible thing to do. However, since we've gone to war, the basic reasons for going to war have been proven to be wrong, and it's not difficult to realize that our continued presence in Iraq is actually being used to cultivate Islamic terrorism. Muslims are known to be very welcoming to guests but ferocious enemies to invaders. Everyday we stay in Iraq we are creating more enemies and more "terrorists," not friends. What for?

How long do we continue wasting borrowed financial resources in a war we should not have started?

Can we see that the political instability we created worldwide interrupted normal oil supplies and production in certain countries, pushed oil prices through the roof, and brought about an economic downturn in the U.S. and many parts of the world?

How can we ever win? When leaders who we identify as "terrorists" issue an audio tape or a video tape or post a speech on a website, which costs them less than $100.00 and forces us to spend billions of dollars on moving battalions of ships, aircraft carriers, tanks, armaments, and troops. It's a ratio in which we cannot win.

How can we ever win? When each soldier costs us at least $100,000.00 per year and our opponents are willing to blow themselves up for the cause they believe in. They are fighting to regain their country and protect their religion and honor, while our soldiers are questioning why they are fighting.

This is a war of ideology; it cannot be won with military might. We are fighting with the wrong armaments. We have to fight with our ideology. Can we show our "enemy" the benefits of our ideology, the true meaning of democracy, freedom of speech, religion, and freedom of movement? Can we give them a taste of equality of sexes, and equality under the law no matter who you are or what race you belong to? Can we have them face their hypocrisy, cruelty, injustice, and intolerance of anything and anybody who does not fit their mold? And then see how their defenses crumble.

Let's use the same armaments they are using; it's a lot more effective and creates lasting friendships and relationships and lets the one with the best ideology win. Not all Muslims are fanatics. It pays to differentiate bad apples from good ones. We might need to make certain adjustments in ours because true Muslims can definitely teach us something about morality and family values.

Staying in Iraq on a war footing is the wrong thing to do. Saddam is gone. Let the Iraqis decide how they want to govern themselves; we can advise them when asked, but we should not force our system down their throats. It won't work. History tells us so.

The $100 billion-plus that we spend in Iraq every year can be used domestically to boost our economy.

SOCIAL SECURITY/MEDICARE IMBALANCE

As we all live longer and the percentage of retired and living Americans increases, who and how are we going to pay the retirement benefits we have been promised?

Better living conditions and medical improvements are prolonging our lives. Isn't it logical that we extend the retirement age to seventy or seventy-two to increase the base of working Americans to be able to support the retired and needy ones? We do not have to wait until the Social Security fund is bankrupt before we take action. The time to act is now. The sooner, the better.

During 2008, the U.S. government will be spending a total of $1,203 billion on Social Security, Medicare, and Medicaid, representing over 41% of the government's budget. At this rate, this percentage will only go higher and squeeze all other sectors of governmental priorities until we reach to a breaking point.

Do we really have to wait until we hit the wall?

REAL ESTATE FORECLOSURES

It's common knowledge that, like many other industries, real estate prices are cyclical. When prices and interest rates are low, many Americans buy real estate primarily as a residence, especially with the tax incentives the government has put in place to promote home ownership. As too many people want to buy and there are no suitable homes available (low supply), prices start creeping up until people can not afford them anymore, then the reverse starts.

T o encourage U.S. economic growth after 9-11, the Fed lowered interest rates to historically low levels, which made homeownership affordable for many Americans. With abundant supply in the pipeline, American households kept buying houses as soon as they were built, many with 5% down or even zero down. It did not matter, because for a period of roughly twenty-four months, prices were going up automatically, building an equity base for homeowners. On top of that, a lot of creative financing instruments were introduced, with teaser rates, very attractive low-interest rates, minimum income verification or documentation, and so on. Accordingly, many buyers who would not have qualified for a loan did and moved in. They were proud owners until rates started adjusting higher, and their payments started increasing to levels they could not afford.

Naturally, real estate ownership is the single biggest investment for the majority of Americans. Protecting that wealth and right is in the interest of all.

For a small fee, FDIC insures depositors at all insured U.S. banking institutions for up to $100,000.00 of their deposits.(limit raised to $250,000.00 since then) Why wouldn't FNMA or Freddie Mac, for a small fee, guarantee the value of a single-family home after a proper and realistic appraisal is done, so that a family's lifetime savings is not wiped out, as well as protect the viability of our financial institutions?

Considering all the historical data we have on real estate prices nationwide, that is not a very difficult task to achieve and a small price to pay to cover down cycles we are experiencing now.

NATIONAL DEBT AND DEFICIT SPENDING

Being an eighteen years ex-banker, I very well know the value of credit and what it can do to promote economic activity.

As of April 2008, the total U.S National debt is $9.5 trillion, which is about $31,000 per person.(As of Sept.2022, our National debt has gone up to $31 trillion representing a $93,000 obligation per person) Total debt currently is 66.5% of the total GNP of $14.3 trillion (As of Sept 2022, our National debt is 140%. Of our $21.7 trillion GDP) When President George W Bush took over the helm, it was $5.769 trillion, and by the end of his term there was a net increase of $4.731 trillion, almost doubling our national debt. This is definitely not a good deed to be remembered by.

Thanks to low interest rates, the interest due on this debt is only $261 billion, which is 9% of the government's $2.9 trillion 2008 budget. (As of 2022, our debt service has gone up to $677 billion representing 12.66% of our National $5.35 trillion annual budget) A mere 1% increase in interest rates would increase the government's debt service by $95 billion/year, which makes you realize that the U.S. government is the best beneficiary of low-interest rates.

The critical question is, what happens to the government's debt service when rates start creeping up to 7, 8, or 9%? What will happen to tax rates, and what services would we be forced to cut or eliminate?

In summary, we are where we are. It's a tough spot, but not the end of the world. Let's face our problems, learn from our mistakes, and start a process of how we can solve our problems. It can be done and should be done, not postponed to the next president or next congress, but now.

WHO DO YOU THINK I AM

(WHO DO YOU THINK WE ARE)

I am an Armenian.

One of those pure-blooded ones

With roots submerged

In the icy peak of Mount Ararat.

So were my parents and grandparents,

So were my wife's parents and grandparents,

And the parents and grandparents of over one hundred generations,

Not that I have anything against mixing with other nationalities;

On the contrary,

Studying international business management

And doing business in my field

Has allowed me to appreciate and admire

The strengths of various nationalities.

But I am, who I am,

An Armenian by birth.

I know that for many, the purity of my blood means nothing,

I know the ranks of such Armenians are diminishing

In this shrinking and borderless world,

I even might be the last of such an Armenian in my own family,

But I am, who I am,

And I am proud of who I am.

As an Armenian,

My ancestors were the first to recognize Christ

As the only son of God.

And I ponder about the geographic location of Armenia,

And our much larger and powerful neighbors

Surrounding us throughout history,

And the willpower and determination we needed

To sustain our Christian faith.

I read about the lengthy persecution, torture, and massacres,

That our grandparents experienced,

And a majestic veneration builds in me . . .

Nothing can make me more proud,

Nothing can make us more proud,

To be an Armenian:

A member of the first Christian nation in the world.

That's who I am,

That's who we are.

I have been tested with fire,

And we have been tested with fire.

Pain and suffering has been our companion for over twenty-six centuries.

But

Look at me,

Look at us;

I have survived

We have survived.

I know what it takes to start all over again,

We know what it takes to start all over again.

To start from nothing,

Create it,

Build it,

Nourish it,

And see it all plundered,

But have the courage to start again,

And again,

And again,

Because

That's who I am

That's who we are

Armenians.

SECTION IV

PEARLS OF WISDOM

WHAT DO YOU SEE?

Look carefully.

What do you see?

Many look and see nothing,

Few can pick up a little dot out of place in a scene,

Others see the horror in what they are observing,

But some rare souls,

See hope, love, and beauty;

It's all in the mindset,

A matter of perspective.

THE CANVAS OF OUR LIVES

Every day,

The way we act,

The way we decide,

The way we speak,

The way we listen,

The way we react,

The way we love,

The way we care,

The way we disregard,

The way we treat others,

Paints a vivid brushstroke on the canvas of our life.

Once in a while,

It would be interesting to step a few yards away

From the canvas picture we have painted of our life,

And ask ourselves,

Are we proud and happy,

Of our life's picture,

On the canvas that we have painted?

FEEL BETTER TODAY

Do you want to be happy today?

Make someone else happy.

Do you want to be with a friend today?

Call or visit a friend.

Do you want to talk with someone,

About all that is bothering you?

Listen to someone else's problems.

Do you want someone to pray for you?

Pray for someone by name.

Act on it.

Go ahead, do it;

You will feel a lot better today.

DIFFERENTIATE YOURSELF

Knowing how to differentiate yourself

From thousands of others

Who do something similar to what you do

Is the key to success.

Do you have something unique,

That only you have?

A unique flavor,

A unique taste,

A unique product,

A unique concept,

A unique solution,

A unique look.

So that you can stand out,

So that you can disregard your competition,

Because

They simply do not have what you have.

Find your uniqueness, and

Success will be waiting at your front door.

ALL THAT TIME IS GONE

Tick-Tok-tick-Tok,

Seconds followed each other to complete a minute,

Tick-Tok-tick-Tok,

Minutes followed each other to complete an hour,

Tick-Tok-tick-Tok,

Hours followed each other to complete a day,

Tick-Tok-tick-Tok,

Days followed each other to complete a week,

Tick-Tok-tick-Tok,

Weeks followed each other to complete a month,

Tick-Tok-tick-Tok,

Months followed each other,

And the year is gone . . .

Wow . . . How quickly it all went! What did I do during all that time?

I had twelve months,

I had 52 weeks,

I had 365 days,

I had 8,760 hours,

I had 525,600 minutes,

I had 31,536,000 seconds,

And it is all gone . . .

All that time is gone . . .

Did I make it count?

Tick-Tok-tick-Tok . . .

TIME

God created the universe in seven days.

He created you and me in his image,

And you are the best thing He created,

He gave you authority over all his earthly creations,

How many seven days have you had so far?

There are fifty-two weeks, with seven days each in a year,

You do the math,

So, what have you done with your time?

If you look back at what you have done with your time? Are you impressed?

Besides helping yourself,

How many people have you helped?

Have you made any positive contributions to other people's lives?

If you are not happy with what you have done so far,

You always have tomorrow.

Decide to start right now,

Because you still have time.

You still have a whole lifetime:

A lot of multiple seven days,

To create whatever your heart and mind desire.

In our average lifetime of seventy years,

We have three thousand, six hundred and forty seven-day cycles.

Our Lord created the whole universe in seven days,

He created you in His image,

What are you waiting for?

Use your remaining time well.

PEN & PAPER

How are you, my good old friends?

You both are dear to my heart;

I always miss and look forward to your visits to articulate what I feel.

I know there are a lot of new ways,

I pads, I phones, tablets, laptops,

Which can do what you do,

But with a lot faster, easier and superior functionality.

But you know me,

I am old-fashioned.

I use the playful pen in my fingers

To write, scratch, re-write, re-scratch,

On a piece of paper, then I

Throw the page away and start all over again.

This better translates my mental turmoil,

My inner emotions, insights, feelings, and thought processes,

And creates the right environment for raw poetry to flow.

So, thank you, my good old friends,

Don't delay your spontaneous visits,

I will always keep a spare set of pen & paper next to my bed and
inside my car,

Your presence and company mean so much,

In bringing peace, sanity, and harmony, in this busy life of ours.

CONSISTENCY

I like the freedom and variety the ladies take with their appearance,

Their hair,

Their eyes,

Their face,

Their dresses,

Their perfumes,

Their shoes,

Their purses & belts,

Their necklaces, earrings and bracelet sets

From top to bottom, they try

Different shades, colors, and scents,

To fit whatever occasion is called for.

While we as men are stuck with the same old,

Same look, with little change.

Consistency?

Or,

A different coordinated collage of the day?

I do not know which one is right or wrong.

I know, I personally am stuck in being boringly consistent,

However, I do enjoy and appreciate the tasteful variety in appearances of females,

After all, that is what makes them desirable.

DO NOT COMPLICATE YOUR LIFE

As we go through life,

As we face situations or choices on our path,

Before we decide one way or another,

Stop for a moment and ask yourself a wise question.

Will the choice I make, or

will the decision I make

Complicate my life,

Or simplify it?

It is usually not very difficult

To mentally go through this exercise.

Analyze the choices you have in front of you,

And if you think you will complicate your life,

Don't go there.

If the choice will simplify it,

You have the green light to go forward.

Whatever you are facing now,

Ask yourself, will it complicate or simplify your life?

Decide accordingly.

You will have a happier life,

When you keep your life as simple as you can.

BE THE BEST YOU CAN BE

2016 TIME magazine's May 2-9 issue,

Has a very valuable article,

About "The 100 Most Influential People in the World."

With Priscella Chan and Mark Zuckerberg of Facebook on the front cover.

As I read about TIME'S rendition of who they are and why they were chosen.

I asked myself, *Who amongst the 100 I could take up as my hero?*

As I read through them one by one, I came to the only sane conclusion:

I WANT TO BE THE BEST I CAN BE.

I did not want to copy or imitate anyone,

Because God created me to be me,

I hope you feel the same about yourself.

BE THE BEST YOU CAN BE.

THE RIGHT WAY TO ACT

Act justly and fairly,

Act wisely,

Act calmly,

Act thoughtfully,

Act patiently,

Act decisively,

Act until you accomplish the task at hand,

Act with love and compassion,

Act such that you will not regret your actions later,

Act with the full knowledge that God is watching.

IT'S ALL IN THE MINDSET

How do you feel?

How do you see things all around you?

How do you act and react?

How much positive energy do you possess?

How much can you accomplish?

How do you face your daily chores and unpleasant events?

How many tasks can you accomplish every day?

How high can you climb?

How much can you achieve?

It's all in your mindset,

And the switch is in your hand.

Turn your switch on,

Start your engine.

HAVING A CLEAR OBJECTIVE

I like to have a clear objective,

A well-defined list of what I want to achieve in life.

I do not like having hidden agendas,

People who I deal with should know where I stand on certain
issues.

What do I consider to be right?

What do I consider to be wrong?

What is acceptable?

What is not?

Things are pretty well defined in my mind,

Primarily based on Biblical principles.

Naturally, I am also a guy with common sense,

Who is willing to listen to legitimate modern ideas,

I do not like double, triple, or quadruple masks,

Trying to fit in whatever environment I am in.

Even though I play chess well , and can easily

Plan two, three, and four moves beyond any opponent,

I still prefer being straightforward.

I speak my mind quite clearly,

You definitely will know where I stand on the issues at hand,

If I have to address or attack an issue,

I always come from the front.

You will feel and see me coming

With full force and everything I have.

I will always fully explain why I act a certain way;

There are no side deals in my vocabulary,

And I do not use and or sacrifice others for my benefit.

I fight my own battles,

And if I lose or fail,

I'll try to understand what happened and why.

If deep in my heart, the Lord convinces me that my position was right,

No matter the cost,

I will gather all my resources, and I will come back.

I do not get frightened or feel in despair,

If a mountain has to be taken,

Great obstacles have to be eliminated.

High goals have to be accomplished. I will not rest,

I will not succumb,

I will not get tired,

Until the objectives are achieved,

So help me, God.

WHAT A YEAR 2010!

Soon another year is coming to an end,

Two-thousand ten will be no more,

And what a year it's been.

Many, many times, it has been depressing to watch television,

Read newspapers, or go through internet headlines,

Learning of ongoing bloodshed and suicide bombers,

Ripping apart indiscriminately in Iraq, Pakistan, and Afghanistan.

Thousands and thousands of real estate foreclosures,

High delinquency of credit card debt,

Historically unheard of high unemployment rates and pink slips,

Widespread fraudulent activities in private and governmental agencies,

The continuing saga of importing much more than exporting,

Resulting in an unhealthy situation of shutting down our manufacturing base,

Sending our jobs overseas and weakening our US economy,

Gradual devaluation of our currency,

Gold and silver, as well as many other commodity prices, are soaring,

Ongoing FED bailout of major financial and industrial institutions,

Euro-zone meltdown in Greece, Iceland, Portugal, Spain, Ireland, and the next in line,

Upside-down mortgages,

High commercial and residential vacancy rates,

Greedy and clueless elected officials, whose main goal seems to be

Securing and continuation of their lucrative pay, pensions, and perks,

Rather than preparing the right economic and legal environment,

To improve the standard of living of the general public,

Horrifying months-long oil spill in the Gulf,

Resulting in devastating ecological oceanic damage,

Not to mention the cruel loss of life and industrial shutdowns,

State and municipal governments bloated with red ink,

Unimaginable piling up of federal government debt and deficits.

We are watching with anxiety in our hearts and minds,

Our Federal Reserve Bank is printing billions and billions of IOUs,

Dollars that are your and my debt,

Thirteen trillion dollars and counting of government burrowing

Which we will never be able to pay back,

Just to make sure that for now

They can keep the whole country from crumbling.

So,

How was your year?

How are your nerves?

Are you holding up?

How were your health, family, job, and children?

I assume you had your share of inner turmoil,

Unresolved problems and sleepless nights,

Are you worried and scared of what's to come?

How will this nightmare ever end?

Will the sun ever rise again?

When will I feel secure and peaceful again?

Good questions.

I hope deep in your heart that you know the answer,

It's quite simple; it's in Psalm 23,

"Though I walk through the valley of the shadow of death,

I will fear no evil, for You are with me,

Your rod and staff, they comfort me."

Another verse to remember during this holy season comes from Isaiah 9-6,

"For unto us, a child is born,

Unto us, a child is given,

And the government will be upon His shoulder,

And His name will be called,

Wonderful, Counselor, Mighty God,

Everlasting Father, Prince of peace."

Absorb these verses, and feel the comfort and healing they provide.

Our heavenly Father is in control,

All the anxieties we face today will just be a memory tomorrow,

The immense personal, state, national and international difficulties,

We are facing today, are just trivial details, for the Creator of our universe,

Our earth, with its over six billion inhabitants,

Is only a little drop within God's universe,

If He is capable of coordinating and managing billions of stars with all of their planets,

What are we getting worried about?

How daunting or large are our problems?

Yes, the sun will rise again, so get ready,

Roll up your sleeves,

Gather all your energy for smarter and longer work,

So we can face our challenges head-on.

OUR DESTINY IS IN OUR HANDS,

So, welcome the new year.

It will be a tough year,

And it may be scarier than 2010.

But one we can face with peace and courage,

One, with God's guidance, we can overcome.

HAVE A MERRY CHRISTMAS AND A HAPPY NEW YEAR.

ACTION-REACTION

In human relationships,

Every action

Produces a reaction.

Every day, the individuals we deal with

Act a certain way,

And their action produces a reaction from us.

It is good to remember

That we have no control over the action of others,

But how we react totally depends on us.

Examine your reaction.

You sure can have a great influence

On how people interact with you.

Act accordingly.

SLOWING THE PACE

My life is still running on the freeway,

On the far left: the fastest lane possible.

Today, I decided to join my wife while she visited her uncle

At Ararat Home,

An assisted living establishment for elderly Armenians.

We got entertained during lunch by a talented couple.

We enjoyed the company of many who have been,

On the slow lane of life for some time.

I felt wishful anticipation

That someday, the time will come

For me to choose the slow lane,

And enjoy life's beauty through all its stages.

The fast ones,

As well as the slow ones

Coming up on the horizon. Hopefully, the loneliness associated

with the slow lanes

Will not be a factor to worry about.

I do have my pen and pencil as good friends to accompany me,

My wife has her piano,

We are set for the upcoming slow lanes,

But I will be taking the slow lane going there.

PAST DECISIONS

Every day we make a lot of decisions.

Many are automatic and simple,

But occasionally, we are faced with making

An important decision that will impact our lives for years to come.

As the years pass,

We look back and reflect upon

The impact of our past decisions on our lives.

We realize that some of the decisions we have made

With the information, we had at the time.

Or the lack of proper details which we simply missed or ignored,

Turned out to be the wrong decision.

If we are clever and wise,

All past poor decisions

Should act as a perfect learning opportunity.

Actually, the best learning occurs when we get hurt by our own decisions.

DON'T MAKE THE SAME MISTAKES AGAIN.

Keep going,

More and more, you will develop better judgment,

On how to choose from the various alternatives you are facing,

That life sets us on our path.

Wrong decisions in the past will lead us to make the right decisions
in the future.

ORGANIZE & FOCUS

It all starts with me, and it's all my fault.

I have cluttered my life with pages and pages of "things to do,"

Overburdening myself has been my weakness.

God has endowed me with a lot of talents and abilities.

So, I ventured right and left in many directions.

For years, I have donated a large portion of my time

To non-profit organizations,

As a means of thanking the Lord for all the gifts and life He has given to me,

Attending meetings after meetings, sometimes five days a week,

Naturally, as I did that, I delayed or did not process,

All the things I have to do every day,

So, simple tasks started piling up,

My "things to do" list became longer and longer,

And many tasks remained on that list for months and months.

Simply because I had so many things to do,

I could only focus on emergency flare-ups,

Only when I got hit with penalties, late pays, expiration notices,
and so on.

So, enough is enough.

Starting today,

I will learn to say, "No, I do not have time."

To any new commitment, organization, or task that requires
allocation of my time.

I will focus on all the things that are on my plate right now,

And do them one by one starting from the most important,

The most urgent,

And do all my daily tasks.

Do not postpone things that have to be done today. I need to rid of
so much extra baggage I have accumulated and carried for so long,

and simplify my life

By eliminating, cutting, and throwing away all unnecessary tasks
and commitments.

It starts from my office;

I want to be able to see my desk beneath all the envelopes, paperwork, pamphlets, and books.

In the end, I want to look straight in my wife's eyes,

And tell her that I am current with all the things I have to do.

After all, she deserves more of my time, and it will stop her nagging,

She also deserves a lot fewer intrusions and congestion in our daily lives.

I also believe I have done enough good non-profit work,

And deserve a simpler life with fewer commitments,

To enjoy and assimilate all the surroundings that God has created.

It's time to organize,

It's time to focus,

And it's time to enjoy life.

AN OPPORTUNITY

At 1:00 p.m. today

I just finished meeting my IRS auditor and headed back to my office,

Got into my car in the huge parking lot and started backing out,

When a Hispanic lady approached me with a set of jumper cables,

And asked if I could help her start her stalled car.

I had payroll to process for all staff members,

With a lengthy list of urgent matters in my mind.

I sincerely apologized that I did not have time and started driving away,

But before I could leave the parking lot,

I saw the lady in my rearview mirror at a long distance

And my conscience stopped me.

I returned and parked behind her car;

The parking lot was completely full,

And her cable battery jumpers could not reach my car's battery.

I tried to put her car on neutral and move her car to bring it closer to my battery,

But the shifts were locked, and her car would not move.

I noticed three youngsters in the car,

I smiled and inquired if they were praying for help,

They nodded affirmatively,

Within seconds, miraculously, the car owner of the direct next spot,

Came, went inside their car, and drove away,

I immediately drove to that spot and within one minute,

I started her stalled car.

You could not imagine how good I felt,

Considering that my knowledge of car mechanics is embarrassingly primitive.

Thank you, Lord, for the opportunity.

When you have an opportunity to do good work,

Do it.

A WEEKEND REFLECTION

Simplify your life and live in peace and happiness,

By abiding to the following rule:

"Would my wife/husband approve, and be happy and proud

Of what I am about to do?"

If you think the answer to that question is going to be no,

Then don't do it.

Until you have a conversation with your spouse,

Act accordingly.

Real happiness lies in your family,

Focus on your spouse and children,

THE FAMILY UNIT IS LIFE'S PRIZE.

If you have a family in peace,

Everything else will fall in place.

I WONDER

At a certain age in our lifetime,

We start looking back

At the various stages of our lives. All the things we have done,

And all the things we wanted to do, but never had the time to do.

Like a movie screening,

We see the ups and downs of our lives

Come to us, in vivid flashes.

Are you happy with what you see?

When we are no longer around one day,

How will they remember us?

Did you leave any positive imprint behind?

I wonder.

We all wonder.

IF I HAD ONLY KNOWN

"If I had only known" indeed is an interesting remark;

It usually is related to the fact that,

We would have acted differently,

If we knew the resulting outcome of our decision or action,

But that is life,

Many, many times, we have to decide or act with limited information,

Many times with wrong or fabricated information,

Afterwards, we justify ourselves by saying:

"If I had only known."

Tough luck, that's life.

The challenge is to make decisions, or act, with limited information,

And be capable of making the right decision.

God will never say, "If I had only known,"

That's only a human expression.

I hope as years pass by, you use this remark less and less.

DISCERN WHAT YOU SEE

So often, what we see on television or on the internet,

What we hear on the radio or airways,

What we read in newspapers, magazines, and books,

Are photoshopped,

Obvious or subtle paid advertising by an organization,

Nothing to do with truth or reality,

And specially prepared to indoctrinate us and program our minds.

Can we see through the fog?

Can we have enough intelligence?

To differentiate, understand, and grasp,

The real picture or situation we are facing.

God has endowed us with a brain,

To filter what we see, hear, and read.

Do not be part of a blind herd,

Educate yourself to analyze, verify, and re-verify,

To determine the truth, the real intent or picture,

Of what you see, read, and hear.

MAKE SOMEONE HAPPY TODAY

Today is a fresh new day;

Make someone happy today,

Bring a pleasant smile to someone's face,

Give a caring ear to another,

Make them feel that you are there for them,

Make them feel that they are special to you, and

You are praying for them by name.

Who knows? One day,

You might be looking for a person like that,

So, you start being that person,

Today.

TESTING YOUR GOALS

When you look back,

And ask yourself,

Why have you worked for so long?

Why did you give so much of yourself?

Why did you invest so much time, energy, and resources?

And you search and search for an answer,

But can not find a satisfactory response,

Then, realize you are in the wrong endeavor.

You are on the wrong road,

You are wasting your precious time,

Stop the waste and redirect your life by focusing on productive

tasks.

TREASURED MOMENTS

Sometimes, life is condensed,

In mere moments of pure joy,

Distilled seconds of light,

Of music,

Of laughter,

Of thoughts,

Of emotions,

Of love.

Living becomes so worthwhile when I watch a little baby smile,

Talk, walk, fall down, and immediately rise again so naturally.

Captivating our lives, as we witness

A new beginning.

Life is just a constant search for those cherished moments.

The rest is just fluff:

Busy work.

Yes, those few moments,

Everlasting, condensed seconds,

Makes our life's journey

So worthwhile, rewarding, soul-enriching, and meaningful.

YOU GET TIRED

The day will come

When you will get tired of everything and everybody,

Everything will look the same for you,

You will get tired of wearing the forced smiley face,

You will get tired of trusting everyone,

You will get tired of loving everyone and not being loved in return,

You will get tired of helping people who do not appreciate your help,

You get tired even from crying,

You will get tired of life,

You will get tired of seeing the same people every day,

You will get tired of the same streets, homes, rocks, and everything.

You will get tired, but you will continue living.

Do you know why?

Because there are some people who depend on you,

There are some others upon whom you depend on,

You will get tired,

But because of them, you continue living.

Armenian poet Baruyr Sevag 1924-1971

Translated by Ara Assilian

SURROUNDED WITH LOVE

The best way to enrich your inner soul

Is to learn how to love. To see, appreciate, and nurture the beauty

that surrounds us,

To be able to see beyond the superficial and apparent,

Go deep inside, uncover the hidden beauty and talent,

Underneath the surface of the people all around you,

Hold it close to your heart,

And cherish that special privilege of learning how to love.

It's boundless,

It's eternal,

It's all around you.

It's all up to you to see, feel and enjoy,

You have full control;

You have the switch button for love.

Turn it on,

And experience, feel, and radiate the love in your life.

DEFINE WHO YOU ARE

Do you really know who you are?

Do you really know how you have become who you are?

Who were your teachers?

Where did you learn whatever you know?

Who were your friends?

If what you have become was dependent on

A lot of people and circumstances,

And you don't necessarily like what you have become,

Then, what do you want to be?'

Where do you want to go?

What do you want to accomplish?

It is totally up to you.

You are driving your own vehicle;

You are in the driver's seat.

Choose your own destination,

Choose your own direction,

Stop blaming others for the circumstances you are in,

Or the situations you are placed in.

Choose to be in charge of your own life,

So that you can properly define who you are.

<u>WHAT DO YOU THINK OF YOURSELF?</u>

It does not matter what people think of you;

It's what you think of yourself that really matters.

So, discover, educate, and cultivate who you want to be.

Above all, persist and persevere until you find out

Who you really are?

Who you really want to be?

VOICES OF REASON

Scary times we live in;

Too many hostilities happening all at the same time.

Too many riots,

Too many acts of looting,

Too many killings,

And too many radicals,

That run around with sophisticated weapons in their hands,

Filled with hate, anger, and an uncompromising belief

That they are absolutely right,

And the others are definitely wrong and have to be stopped,

They have a willingness to accomplish their heinous objectives,

With whatever it takes.

Burn it down, smash it, break it, let lawlessness reign.

What a waste!

It is time to wake up.

Let us understand that if we continue on this path

We all lose, and no one wins.

We need more voices of reason,

Voices of tolerance and peace,

Let us conquer this inhumane battle of radicalism on all sides.

COMMON SENSE

I value people who utilize common sense

in their daily decision-making process.

To me,

It's an ability to utilize our intellect

To view what's happening all around us,

Analyze all the pros and cons of a given situation,

Use logic,

To analyze what we are reading, hearing, and seeing,

And then reach an informed common sense conclusion.

Using this approach,

I thought I could easily predict a specific outcome,

Of how events will develop and unfold,

Or how majority of people with common sense

Will reach the same conclusion.

However, time and time again,

I started realizing that

My ability to predict, using my common sense approach

Is not working accurately.

I had to ask,

What is wrong with my common sense approach?

I realized that my mind, any mind,

Is a very sophisticated processor of information.

Even though many of us receive the same information and data,

How our individual brains process that knowledge

Within our existing storage memory

Could be significantly different.

My common sense analysis and decision-making process

Could be a lot different than someone else's common sense.

Our world is getting very complex.

The information, or misinformation, is so difficult to differentiate.

Common sense is out,

Chaos is in;

We just need common sense to learn how to live in it.

RELATIONSHIPS

Human relationships,

Business relationships,

Country relationships,

Regional relationships,

Are always a two-way street.

A one-way relationship is always short-term; it will not last.

If you want a lasting relationship, always keep that in mind,

If you have nothing to offer to another person, do not expect
anything from them.

If you want something from a person, you have to learn what to
give in return.

In the long run,

The give and take equation has to be balanced if you want it to last.

I rub your back, and you rub mine.

This is how it has been from time eternal,

This is how it is between husband and wife,

Employers and employees, teachers and students, producers and consumers, sellers and buyers,

As well as international governmental relationships,

A two-way equilibrium of give and take, never a one-way street.

The only exceptions to this rule are our relationship with our Father, Creator,

Who gives us so abundantly,

With the hope that

We learn to do the same to our children and not expect anything in return.

JUDGING ONE'S CHARACTER

As an ex-banker,

Analyzing, reviewing, and judging a borrower's character

Was a very important task for me,

Especially as the main credit analyst and manager of the bank

In their international credit department.

A borrower's character is a key consideration,

In determining if the funds you are lending are safe.

During my eighteen-year-long banking career,

Only once have I miscalculated or misjudged a borrower's character.

Outside of banking, however,

So many instances, way too many times,

I have been wrong in analyzing and judging,

The character of people I have associated with.

It takes time to really know someone;

How do they think?

How do they behave?

How do they act and react?

How dependable and truthful are they?

One sure thing I have learned,

Is not to be hasty in judging someone else's character.

Time and time again,

When you get disappointed in discovering

Unacceptable behavior and characteristics

Of people you are associated with,

You realize that we are all faulty human beings.

Get out of the business of judging any one's character.

Only God can judge someone accurately,

Let Him be the final judge.

SECTION V

PEARLS OF FAMILY AND LOVE

LIFE WORTH LIVING

To live without love, is no life,

To live without love, is constant torture,

To live without love, is experiencing hell,

To live with love, is life worth living

I WILL SING

I sing with joy, I sing with sadness,

I sing with boundless vigor, I sing with silent pain,

I wonder where I am heading. with these happy and tearful songs,

Sometimes determined and sometimes uncertain.

Every time my soul is thrilled,

When my heart is delighted with a flaming love,

And my emotions take flight in the skies above,

I sing, I sing just like a nightingale.

Every time when my soul is saddened,

My heart is in anguish and hopeless despair,

When my mind earnestly seeks a little light from its surrounding
darkness,

I sing. I sing with a painful heart.

And I will be singing for a long time to come,

I will spread my song to all nations afar,

Until the whole world sings together,

The song of love: the only song of our existence.

High school teenage romance from 1967

THE FIRST CLICK

It is so vivid in my mind,

As though it happened yesterday.

I still remember coming down the steps of Omar Khayam restaurant:

A reputable formal dining eatery in San Francisco.

It was my last day of being the captain of the restaurant.

I just had graduated from San Francisco State University,

And was planning to start full-time with Wells Fargo Bank.

I came down the stairs

From a relatively dark entrance,

As I landed on the main floor,

There she was,

Next to the cashier's podium,

With a light shining on her face.

On her first day in the restaurant,

Click,

I introduced myself,

And her smiling face was stuck in my heart,

As I sat the dining guests at their tables,

I gravitated myself next to the entrance where she stood.

Click, click.

I hastily planned and invited her,

For a whole week of daily outings together:

A crash course in knowing each other. She said yes to all.

For our camping trip in the Sierras, she wanted to bring along her sister.

No problem, I said.

Mr. Mardigian Jr., the owner's son,

Noticing the sparkle in our eyes

And the percolating chemistry in our body movements,

Encouraged me to invite her to an Armenian banquet/dance,

Happening the next day.

I did,

She said yes

In the banquet hotel elevator.

I dared to hold her hand with so much pride,

As if I was saying, *look who I got,*

Click, click, click.

Within one week, I knew this was it.

I was twenty-four,

I was ready to set the course of my life,

To commit to love and cherish her against all odds,

Two months later, we were engaged on her birthday.

She wanted to make sure I knew what I was doing,

That I was not crazy,

And I told her, yes, I was;

I was crazy in love. Two months after that, we were married.

She had run away, or said no, to so many,

But she said "I do" to me.

Click, click, click, click,

I hit life's lottery,

I hit the jackpot,

A Lifetime front seat of eternal music,

A lifetime of selfless, sacrificial love

It was the best decision I have ever made in life,

For which I am so thankful:

So thankful to my Lord. Here and there, I have made some mistakes,

I know,

But the most important decision of my life;

Choosing my soul mate,

I got it so right

Sooo right.

For our 45th anniversary to my tsakoog.

Jan. 2020

MY PORCELAIN DOLL

I gaze at her from a distance as she plays the piano.

She gracefully bobs her head up and down,

Translating the musical notes to touching and emotional tunes.

The sunlight from the church's stained windows,

Highlights her facial features,

And she looks like a porcelain doll

From where I sit, some fifteen yards away.

Somehow, her physical age and facial features

Disconnect;

The Lord has blessed her with ageless beauty.

I see what a blessed lady looks like,

And I feel so honored to be the primary beneficiary

Of this porcelain doll,

My wife.

THE ALARM CLOCK

In the early morning,

My alarm gives a soft, two-minute warning buzz.

My sleep gets interrupted,

And half asleep, I move my arm around.

I feel her hand next to me,

I put my hand on hers,

And in auto reflex, I start praying.

Feeling my life's umbilical cord next to me.

Then, gracefully, I move my hand all over her warm body,

Making sure that I do not wake her up.

She is mine, all, mine,

And I continue to pray thankfully,

For the treasured gift, my prize

The Lord has given me.

The two minutes pass,

The alarm is now in full force.

With a wake-up like this,

I am ready,

For whatever challenges and opportunities,

The day will bring.

Have a lovely day.

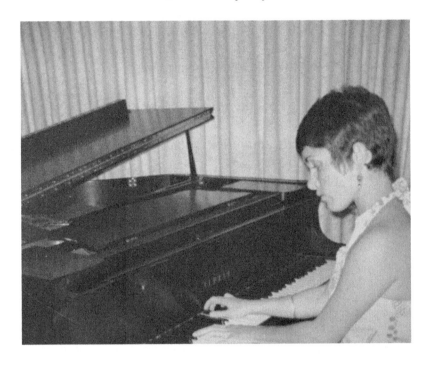

GRATITUDE

How valuable is this?

How do you express the thankfulness in your heart,

For the lifelong gift you have been given?

You look in amazement,

You listen with so much pleasure to your senses,

You admire her natural musical talent,

You appreciate her graceful, emotional interpretations,

Of every note, with such tenderness and class.

You gaze at her whole body movement with a humbling pride,

Realizing, that, for some reason,

You, are the primary beneficiary of this worldly prize.

With utmost gratitude in your heart,

You cry.

FALLING IN LOVE

Falling in love is relatively easy.

Staying in love, however,

Requires a lot of hard work,

Centered around thinking about your soul mate's needs

Before you think about your own.

THE RIGHT DECISION

When you know,

Deep in your heart,

Choosing your soul mate and your spouse;

The most important decision of your life,

You got it right.

Then, embrace her,

Cherish her,

And do not worry about making a few mistakes here and there.

When you have life's foundational decision right,

Who cares about making a few bad decisions?

She will help you to correct them.

REQUIRED BUSY PAPERWORK

Lord, I am so thankful,

For the many blessings,

That you have bestowed upon me.

From my earliest memories of childhood,

There are too many to count.

Many, I have taken for granted,

The biggest blessing of them all,

Is my wife of forty-one years.

Show me, Lord, where I can improve,

Brighten my mind and give me the necessary energy

To do all the required little, busy tasks,

The never-ending paperwork needed while running a business,

That has been out there for some time.

A long time.

Spoiling enjoyable times with my wife and family.

Help me, Lord, to eliminate the obstacles,

Many self-created,

So that we can enjoy the love that You put in our hearts.

LIFE IS GOOD

If you live with love in your heart and mind,

Life becomes so good.

Take love out,

Replace it with hate,

Stir in jealousy,

Mix it with quick anger,

Add a little envy,

With a tad of selfishness,

Flavored with an uncompromising spirit,

And you convert your life into a living hell.

Learn how to share,

Learn how to love,

Learn how to be thankful,

Learn how to forgive,

And see your life blossom.

The quality and goodness of your life,

Is totally, in your hand.

VALENTINE'S DAY

Today is a special day,

We all call it Valentine's Day,

It makes me reflect on memories,

Memories that have been an eternal blessing from our Lord.

For indeed He must have loved me,

Otherwise, why should I be so blessed with love?

So much loved, cherished, and cared for.

I know it was a dicey chance we took,

Some twenty-two years ago,

The odds were definitely stacked against us,

But with joy and tears,

We tied our eternal knot,

And life has been a harmonious paradise ever since.

Don't be mistaken;

It hasn't been all peaceful, happy, and glorious,

For sure, we've had more than our fair share of heartbreaking events,

And an unending barrage of turmoil and temptation all around,

But through it all,

Almost every day,

I've thanked our Eternal Lord,

For blessing me with a loving and loveable wife,

Indeed a better half,

To give me strength when it was impossible to face tomorrow,

To give me hope when it was so hopeless all around,

To give me life when living and waking up, became absolutely meaningless,

To give me love, God's best blessing to mankind.

For all this, I thank my Lord,

I thank Him from the bottom of my heart,

For when we have love in our hearts.

In vain, we look for other treasures,

There is absolutely nothing that can match or replace love.

And darling, you know I am a man of many dreams,

Sometimes, too many lofty and impossible dreams,

But someday, years from now,

If I am ever remembered in kindness and love,

I want to be remembered as a loving husband to my queen Esther,

Since that is the best thing I know how to do.

With love.

Feb 1996

HEAVENLY MELODIES

As I listen to soft melodies

My soul is elevated skyward.

In the middle of a very difficult and depressing week at work,

I am enchanted, grateful, and thankful

To my Lord.

For he knows very well what's going on in my life,

As He has come through so many times before.

I know these difficulties I face will pass.

As I enjoy my cozy surroundings at home,

I again feel so blessed and favored by my Lord,

For giving me a strong and beautiful wife,

Who is so tenacious, supportive, and tolerant,

With endless energy to help and love all her surroundings.

I look at her and admire her

Even after thirty-five years of marriage,

For indeed, the most important decision in life,

I got it right,

My numerous other blunders, well, who cares,

I am not perfect

No one is.

With background music playing and sitting on a rocking chair,

I feel so blessed and thankful.

I am thankful for my son, daughter, and beautiful grandson,

I am thankful to my parents and in-laws for all their love,

Thankful for my relatives close and far,

Thankful for my present and past friends,

Thankful for our health, food, shelter, and beautiful surroundings,

For these are life's blessings

As created and given by God

For His children to cherish and enjoy.

SECOND FIDDLE

My wife has always been first in my life,

As far as I know, I was also first in her life for a brief period of time,

We were married on Jan, 11th, 1975,

Our first son, Shahe was born , on Dec. 28, 1975.

At which time, I had to give up my first priority position to my son,

In three years, our second son; Hrag, was born,

I had to take a further step backward,

Another three years and our daughter Lara was born,

Which was another back step for me,

All throughout, my wife's position never changed with me.

She was always my number one,

But I knew that by the time we stopped having children,

I was fourth on her list.

From my perspective,

This unfair ranking didn't bother me.

I knew my place in her life, and I understood her priorities,

I was a second fiddle for her,

And I obediently waited for my turn to come

When she was ready to disperse her full attention.

Years passed by, my son got married,

And I got my first grandson: Gabriel.

Suddenly, my life's focus changed,

I never knew that a grandson could bring so much happiness,

As I have grown, conquering the world was not a goal for me anymore,

My own priorities and expectations from life have changed,

Being around my grandson was a heavenly joy for me,

It all worked so naturally, like a reflex.

The moment I see him,

My facial muscles relax,

And a big smile takes over my face.

He was a newly discovered love, happiness, and joyful bliss,

Instantly upon sight,

Just like I used to feel every time I saw my wife.

With this change of circumstances,

I had to jokingly confess to my wife, with a grin on my face

"You know, honey,

When I see Gabriel, I immediately smile and relax,

Just like I used to feel when we just got married,

But, you don't have that effect on me anymore,

Gabriel does,

I have been getting the second fiddle treatment from you for years,

Now, get a taste of it,

Because my grandson now, is my new concertmaster,

You are my second fiddle."

My youngest grandchildren Jolene and George

Gabriel's colorful drawing talent

Gabriel coloring Easter eggs with Nani

MY GRANDSON, GABRIEL

My little grandson Gabriel

Has wrapped me around his little finger.

He has a daily expanding vocabulary of animal names,

And shows me with his pointed finger as they come on the
television screen,

Turtle . . . whale . . . seal . . .

Shark . . . rhino . . . dolphin,

Looking at me with such a pleasant smile and pride,

He has a unique childish accent on each animal,

As though he wants to show me how smart he is.

I squeeze this heavenly joy into my chest,

And join the fun of discovering the essence of life:

My first grandson.

How blessed I am,

How happy he makes me feel.

Thank you, Lord, for the opportunity to be a grandpa,

I would not compare it with anything,

It is the best thing that happened to me in a long, long time.

TREASURED MOMENTS

After work, I stopped by my son's house and saw my grandson Gabriel

Watching a National Geographic television program

On sea life-reef life within the 14,000 islands of Indonesia,

Many of which apparently are not inhabited by humans,

But it apparently has abundant and lively sea life.

As I watched in amazement the fabulously beautiful reefs,

And the variety of colorful fish lying within the reefs in egg form

Gradually being transformed into swimming fish,

And intricate film of newly hatched fish's heartbeats,

I was thrilled in amazement to be able to witness and share these moments

With my grandson.

I simply have not seen anything like it before.

Gabriel adores all kinds of animals,

And he prefers to watch, play, and be with animals,

A lot more than watching and playing with other human beings.

What a blessed time,

A beautiful learning experience to treasure and share with my first grandson.

Esther and Shahe

HUSBAND & WIFE VS MOTHER & SON-WHICH ONE IS FIRST?

For over thirty-one years, my son Shahe has been my right hand

While I ran Adin of California.

They usually do not recommend working with your wife in the

same office,

But I did, and seldom had a problem,

They do not recommend working with your son in the same office

For similar reasons,

But I did.

We had a lot of quarrels quite often,

And sometimes in front of employees and customers.

One day it was so intense and extreme that I had to let him go.

I told Shahe never to come back,

Because he made me so angry with his short fuse and disrespectful

language.

After one hour,

I called Esther and told her that I had fired Shahe,

And did not want to see him in the office anymore,

She pointedly asked me, "What did you do?"

"I fired him," I said.

With a very stern voice, she said,

"You go, apologize to him and bring him back to the office,

If you do not bring him back to the office,

Do not come home."

I said, "What did you say?"

She repeated the whole statement again,

For all those who know me,

I do not allow anyone to talk to me that way,

But Esther had it in her to do just that.

I waited for an hour, then went to my son's house.

He was doing some gardening to let some steam out.

I told him,

"Your mom wants me to apologize and bring you back to the office."

He asked,

"My mom wants you to apologize. What about you?"

I said,

"I have nothing to apologize for."

The next day Shahe came back to the office,

And from that day on,

I became a paper tiger,

He knew who made the final decisions, as far as he was concerned,

I am so glad I let my wife have her way,

Since the primary purpose of my life is,

"My children's happiness is my happiness, and their failures are
my failures."

Esther had the guts to put her foot down;

I am so proud and happy she did.

SPOUSAL ARGUMENT

Yesterday, while I was driving home with my wife,

We argued for the fourth time

About two pieces of costume jewelry,

That I purchased for her and my daughter last week

While I was attending a nonprofit organization luncheon.

They were two ornate necklace and earring sets

That I felt would look complementary

For the two important ladies in my life.

She asked how much I paid for them,

And unfortunately, I told her how much I paid.

She gave me a lengthy lecture, saying that downtown

She could have purchased the same sets for a fraction of that price.

I told her I wanted to please and surprise her and my daughter,

Besides, the proceeds were going for a good cause and institution

That we both admire and support.

Still, for the fourth time in one week,

She wanted to hammer me with the fact that I overpaid,

So, I've had it,

I raised my voice thunderously, and

Stopped the constant nagging for something so trivial to me,

All night at home, we didn't talk

She slept before I did, so I received no "good night."

The next morning, I woke up and left the house early

While she was sleeping.

On the way to work

I was listening to a beautiful piano piece,

And I was visualizing how Esther would be playing it.

How she would move her hands, her upper body, and head.

Immediately,

Strong emotions overtook my body,

And my eyes got wet.

I wiped my tears, picked up the phone, and called my wife.

"Tsakoog (Darling),

I am sorry for screaming at you yesterday."

"I am sorry for nagging you about it," she replied,

Harmony was back, and my day will be okay.

I simply cannot function if I hurt my wife in any way

CHERISH THE BEAUTY

The years pass by,

We naturally age,

And new generation blossoms.

Yesterday's young children,

Grow up to be handsome and pretty teenagers.

Life circulates,

And new beginnings are everywhere.

Young adults of a few years back

Now have several babies of their own.

The process is just fine;

Deep in my heart, however,

There is a strong desire and yearning

For the Lord to stop the ticking clock,

Or even better,

Rewind for another ride.

Way from the beginning,

So that this time,

I cherish and float in all this beauty,

Life, our life, yours and mine,

That God has so graciously given to us to enjoy.

LIFE'S CYCLE

Life is a cycle.

It turns, and time passes.

I enjoy and love watching

Children and teenagers grow up to be

So handsome, pretty, and glamorous.

A new and colorful generation is growing up.

As we age and mature,

Going through life's cycle,

Deep inside me, however,

A small desire and a fervent wish,

For a second chance.

To go through the ride one more time.

This time a lot wiser,

To re-live and have a little more fun,

A little more time to smell the roses,

Just like my wife does so naturally and with such ease,

Giggling, befriending, and laughing with all age groups,

Truly feeling like she is of the same age,

Like one of the kids.

It doesn't matter how old the other person is,

She has a talent, a gift, so admirable to watch and cherish.

Zoey, Jolene and Georgig

Life enriching embrace from my youngest grandchild, Georgig, an
irreplaceable prize

NORMAL CHILDHOOD

I was born in 1950.

My childhood and teenage years occurred during the 50s and 60s,

In Damascus-Syria first, then Beirut, Lebanon, after I was ten years old,

I was raised in a very loving Armenian Christian family,

Both my parents' families came from Turkish Anatolia,

After the Armenian Genocide of 1915 by the Turks.

My parents were married for fifty-seven years,

Until my mom passed away when she was ninety-four.

During the last four years of her life,

My mom was immobilized and in bed ,

My dad, at the ripe ages of ninety-four to ninety-seven,

Took complete responsibility and care of my mom,

He would not allow any nurse to touch her,

Taking care of my mom was his loving, sacrificial duty until her last breath.

When she passed away,

He lost his reason to live.

He followed her within three months.

All throughout their lives,

I have never seen them quarrel,

I am sure they did, but never in front of me.

From day one, I knew they loved me, and they would do anything for me.

Even though we were relatively poor,

I never felt deprived of anything,

The bountiful, loving family environment made material things secondary.

When I started my own family,

My parents' presence in my house was such a blessing,

It was so wonderful to watch the joy in their eyes,

While they helped me and my wife to raise our children.

Now, I've been married for forty-five years already,

And enjoying the blessings of grandchildren.

Like my parents did to me, I am trying my best to provide

A normal loving childhood for my own grandchildren,

But I look around and wonder,

How can I define a normal childhood today?

What was normal during my childhood

Is sure not normal anymore.

I consider myself to be open-minded.

Having lived in California for the last fifty-one years,

I sure have seen a lot of change,

Today, I wonder, who can define a normal childhood?

Who can define a normal family?

A marriage, till death do us apart, is not normal anymore.

It's a rarity.

How can children apprehend and normalize?

Second-fiddle love of a stepmom, stepdad,

Or stepbrothers and sisters

Rationalize and normalize the constant and ongoing emotional
complex relationship tensions,

Within this family unit.

Of course, we also have other versions of continuously changing
modern families.

If I am so confused and worried at my age,

With all the knowledge and understanding I have,

I wonder how young children process the lack of any norms.

Where anything and everything is acceptable,

Where love, commitment, and compromise

Are so conditional on bilateral material benefits.

The confusion created in a child's mind,

The lack of some specific norms,

What is right? What is wrong?

What is allowed behavior? And what is not allowed behavior?

What can they watch, read or listen to? What can't they?

The created chaos in a child's mind scares me to death.

A child's brain is like wet clay:

It molds, absorbs, and copies what it sees, what it feels, what it experiences,

If it sees and feels love, it will learn how to love,

If it sees and feels a lot of disharmony and discord,

That's what it will absorb.

All these abnormalities make me realize that

Only God can manage the created human mess,

Only God can bring some sense and order to a family's life,

Only God's love can bring hope to the survival of our children,

And bring normalcy to a child's life.

AMAZINGLY, HE DOES THAT ON AN ONGOING BASIS.

FATHERS' DAY

On this Father's day,

We come to you, O Lord,

Father of all fathers,

Father of all mothers,

Father of all human beings, young and old,

You created us with Your image,

You created us and gave us the privilege

Of experiencing, living, and feeling what it means to be a father.

Thank you for the love, patience, and forgiving spirit

That You've endowed us with,

To do the best we can,

To be an exemplary father to our children,

We learned all that from You, O Lord,

Yes, many times we have failed in our duties,

But, we are here to learn from the Father of all,

Teach us, guide us,

To be the best fathers

We could ever be.

With Shahe, Lara and Garo Atachian-my son-in-law

TO MY SON & DAUGHTER

On this Fathers' day,

I want to express my greatest pride, love, gratitude, and admiration

For the way you've grown up.

I thank you for your love and affection.

I thank you for all that you've done to make this a happy family.

I know I could have been a better father,

I could have spent more quality time with you,

And I could have done more pleasant, memorable, and enjoyable activities with you.

I didn't,

I was always so busy,

With so many "worthwhile" or not so worthwhile causes,

Which took so much of my time.

God made me a generous person with tiding my time and knowledge,

A little too DOHMOUNI (genuine) Armenian,

I wasted so many evenings every week on school boards, church boards,

Various and numerous Armenian, political, and professional organizations,

All at your expense.

I was also chasing material wealth

To safeguard a better future for the whole family,

I did not want you to experience the maternal depravity I grew up with.

At this point, I realize I did not have a proper balance;

Please forgive my shortcomings.

If anything, learn from my faults and do better with your children.

I already see Shahe is becoming such a good dad to Gabriel

It makes me proud.

I love you both.

Many times, Mom put all three of you ahead of me.

She had all the right to do so,

Because she carried you for nine months.

But you have my blood and sperm,

For better or worse, you have and are, part of me,

I love you with all my heart,

Your happiness is my happiness,

And your sorrow is mine also.

Your success in life or shortcomings are also mine,

I just wish Hrag would have been with us to enjoy this special Fathers' day,

And Lara, I am impressed with Garo, my son-in-law,

He carries the same name as my brother;

His last name means fire, just like Hrag.

Also, I am sure learning to admire his strict character and work ethic,

May the Lord watch over all of you and guide you for the rest of your days,

I hope you know, you have the best mom the Lord can provide,

She will die for you and protect you as a lion would.

At the end of the day,

Family is the most important entity that God created.

Family life, under our Creator's umbrella,

Will provide the best reason and meaning for our being alive.

Seek it, and enjoy its blessings.

You can already taste it with my grandson, Gabriel,

After sixty, it sure brings so much pleasure to my life.

I am patiently waiting for more,

So, hurry up, and get moving.

With fatherly love.

Archbishop Yeprem Dohmouni, Primate of Syria from 1921 to 1946. One of five candidate archbishops to be Catholicos for the House of Cilicia during the 1946 election. He removed his candidacy for health reasons and died the same year. The insert is with Armenian community leaders in Syria in the 40s.

My parents: Hrair and Nevair Assilian

Lara and Garo's wedding

Esther with five grandchildren

WHAT DOES IT TAKE TO HAVE A HAPPY AND LONG MARRIAGE?

On the Occasion of my Daughter's Wedding

December 30, 2012

Come January, Esther, and I would have been married for thirty-eight years. Wow, how fast time flies. My parents were happily married for fifty-eight years until death took them apart. My wife's parents were married for sixty-three years until death took them apart. Yet the national average in the US for married life is just 7.8 years, with more than half of marriages heading for divorce. Going through two, three, four, or five marriages is becoming more normal, especially in California. So, the question is, what does it take to have a long and happy marriage? This, of course, is an important subject for me today, because my only darling daughter Lara (who we named after Dr. Zhivago's Lara), is getting married to Garo, my son-in-law. From the bottom of my heart, I want them to have what I have.

Let me enumerate certain aspects of married life that have worked for me; this is not based on psychologically and scientifically studied experimentations; rather, it has simply worked for me. Maybe I am setting a high bar for my daughter and son-in-law, but in my book, they deserve it.

1-My first lessons about married life came from my parents. They talked several times about how they had been introduced by their elder relatives, but not much about romantic and burning desires; they did not have to. All I had to do was observe and see their highest love and respect for each other. My mother's name was Nevair (meaning a gift), and she indeed was my dad's gift. I have never seen them fight. We were three brothers, Harout, Garo, and me, the youngest. Before getting married, my dad was a barber in Argentina, but once he got married in Damascus and later on moved the whole family to Beirut-Lebanon, he became a blue collar factory worker with very meager financial means. The 300.00 Lebanese pounds per month that he earned was supposed to cover rent for a one-bedroom apartment at two hundred Lebanese pounds, and the rest was supposed to feed a family of five. My mom was a highly sought-after seamstress, and she helped with her occasional earnings. Even though we had so little, I have never felt poor; my mom always made sure that we were properly dressed, and we have never gone hungry at the Assilian family. Deep in my heart, I knew they loved me to death; they would do absolutely anything for their kids. I had the honor and pleasure of having them around my family right after we got married, to help me raise my kids until they both passed away. During my mom's last years, she could not move. She had to be fed in bed, changed, and cleaned in bed for four years. My dad would not trust anyone with that task; it was his sacred duty, and he did it valiantly from the age of ninety-three to ninety-seven. When she passed away, he insisted on an archbishop conduct the funeral ceremony in honor of his uncle, Archbishop Yeprem Dohmouni, who was instrumental in bringing my dad from Argentina and asking him to marry my mom. When his reason to live went to heaven, he passed away a few months afterwards. Yes, whatever I've learned about loving my wife, I owe it to my dad; he was an excellent example for me.

Garo and Lara, you both come from loving families. Look at your parents' marriage, copy and improve upon whatever good characteristics you have seen in their marriage, and disregard the negatives.

2-I treat my wife as my prize in life, just like my dad did. I earnestly want to show her off on a pedestal. If she looks good, I look good. If she is happy, I am happy. Garo, I am sure you have already found out that Lara is indeed a prize. She has the biggest giving heart that

I know in a lady. She would give more than 100% to the people she loves.

Finding the right soul mate and spouse is the biggest prize of our lives, so be proud of each other, and do not be embarrassed by showing each other off.

3-Several times a week, I put my hand on my wife early in the morning or before going to bed and pray for her. I thank the Lord for giving her to me. I thank Him for seeing me fit to deserve this fabulous gift. Learn how to do this, and see your love and appreciation of each other grow.

Being thankful to the Lord for what you have, each other, every day, is a joy because nobody knows how many years, months, or days we will have. Enjoy each day to the fullest.

4-I have always been the first in my class. I came to California in 1969 when I was only nineteen, worked my way through college, got an MBA degree in international finance, and by the age of twenty-six, I was managing Wells Fargo Bank's International Credit Department. I headed a department of twenty analysts reviewing the bank's international exposure. It was hard for me to learn the art and humility of saying, "I am sorry, honey, I made a mistake." A happy marriage always requires an attitude of first saying you are sorry and first forgiving, even when you know, deep in your heart, you have done nothing wrong. Always treat your marriage more important than your individual self. Learn this, and you will have a happy life.

If you hurt each other during the day or had a fight or disagreement, do not sleep until you say I am sorry to your spouse. Now, I know I do not have a perfect score here, I try, but I think overall that my score here is better than my wife's. For some reason, ladies keep a long grudge.

5-I met my wife by coincidence. I had just received my bachelor's degree from San Francisco State and was planning to do my MBA in International Finance part-time. While I was in college, one of the three part-time jobs I had was a matre di in a classy Middle Eastern/Armenian restaurant called Omar Khayam in San Francisco. Once I got my bachelor's degree, Wells Fargo Bank, where I was working part-time, offered me a full-time job as a credit analyst. Accordingly, I let Mr. Mardigian know, the owner of Omar Khayam, that I had to stop working within a week. On my last day our regular cashier called in sick, and the manager called in Esther, a piano teacher by profession, as a temporary replacement to fill in for that day. That's all it took. As I was seating the dining guests at their tables and coming back to the entrance where Esther was sitting, I tap-danced my way over to her and planned a whole week of dates, events, activities, and excursions. By the end of the first week, my booty was in the bag. Within two months, we were engaged. In the next two months, we were married. I was only twenty-four, and by the end of the first year, my first son, Shahe, was born. You see, I don't mess around. The initial spark happened when I first saw her coming down the steps of the restaurant, and her smiling face enchanted me. The most important decision in my life was marrying my wife, which happens to be the best decision I've made. I feel truly blessed. I hope and wish both of you would be able to say that ten, twenty, or thirty years from now.

You were introduced to each other by a friend. The spark that was ignited in you is precious. Keep it alive. You just started; there is so much of each other that you have yet to discover. Take your time, and enjoy the process.

6-Learn to love your spouse more than you love yourself. It takes time to change your habits. When it comes to clothing, food, shelter, recreation, travel, and so on, think about your spouse first, then yourself. In the end, you will learn to treat yourself last. Your wife, your kids, and you get whatever is left if any, and that's how it is best.

Until today, you individually were the most important thing in your lives. After today, a process of migration starts towards marriage and then a family, during which your ego will diminish, and the family will be the most important thing in life.

7-A marriage is like a line between Point A and Point B, a line between you and your wife. In order to form a strong foundation, you have to connect to Point C directly in the center and form a triangle between you, your spouse, and the Lord. With this Trinity, you will form a family. Invite the Lord in your union; make him an integral part of your family. Have His love for both of you flow freely in your house, and watch your family glow.

As husband and wife, you can plan all you want, but it is very important to seek and ask. "Lord, what plans do you have for our marriage?" Pray and seek guidance from our Heavenly Father. He will show you the way.

8-We are all imperfect human beings. We all have faults, we are good at certain things, and we are pretty bad at others. When you look at each other, always see the positives and disregard the negatives. Remember that emphasizing and reinforcing what is good in you will take you a long way to happiness.

A kind and encouraging word will generate tremendous positive results. Be generous in praising each other.

9-Never, never, never put down your spouse in public. If you have something negative to say, talk about it privately in your bedroom and keep it there.

10-Understand clearly that there is no perfect marriage; that only happens in the movies. You are two human beings with two distinct mindsets. At some point, the honeymoon period will be over, and then you have to learn the art of compromise. Until now, you; were the focus of your universe. Everything orbited around your own needs. Now, you have another person to think about and have to learn how to give in. If you are too rigid on insisting on your own way all the time, the marriage will not last.

11-I do not believe in "this is mine and that is yours"; for example, "my checking account, your checking account." When we got married, it was very simple. We both had nothing, except she had a grand piano. I firmly believe in one pot, and whatever we do, we have, we purchase, we own it 50/50. I know this is rather old-fashioned, but it has worked for me perfectly. As a matter of fact, if my wife ends up with everything we have and I end up with nothing, I will still be a happy man because she is my better half.

12-No couple knows 100% what is stored for them in the future. I am sure you will have many happy days, as well as sad and stressful ones in years to come. Your love for each other will be tested in unexpected ways, and I know about this firsthand when the Lord gave us our second son, Hrag, who could not walk, talk, see, hear, or eat. He was destined to stay in bed for thirteen difficult years, but through him, God redefined the meaning of love in our lives and taught us a primary and most important lesson in life. NEVER GIVE UP ON THE LORD BECAUSE HE WILL NEVER GIVE UP ON YOU. HE WILL ALWAYS PROTECT YOU AND WILL NOT GIVE YOU SOMETHING YOU WILL NOT BE ABLE TO HANDLE. HE WILL ALWAYS BE THERE FOR YOU. Cherish the opportunity of life's difficulties and allow the Lord to chisel and bring out the diamond that you both have in your hearts.

13-Keep it simple. Do not complicate your own lives by having grand material goals to achieve. Of course, this is 180 degrees different from what I felt when I was your age. Even from my high school years, I remember having five-year plans, ten, fifteen, and twenty-year plans, all with numerical numbers attached to them with a straight lineup. Well, life is never a straight line up, and building material blocks of wealth will never bring you happiness. On the contrary, it will be fraught with headaches. So, keep it simple, small, and beautiful, and be satisfied with what you have. Most of all, you have each other. That's a reward many people do not have.

14-Let the music play. One of the great joys of my marriage was the fact that I always felt like I had a front seat in a concert hall. Many times as I was studying or working in my office at home, Esther would be playing just outside in the living room. I come out, sometimes sing a song with her, kiss her, embrace her, joyfully fondle with her, all on a prepaid plan at no cost. Can you imagine I do not have to pay a penny? She already got everything I have. One specific night as I was working in my office at home, I heard the piano playing, but realized it wasn't Esther. I looked outside, and it was my daughter Lara. Oh, what a joy that was. I kissed her, went back to my office, and wrote the following few lines.

Play for me, my loves,

Lift my soul to the heavens above,

Oh, how sweet it all sounds,

The melody of the music is divine.

What a blessing this all is,

First, it was my wife,

Enticing my spirits with her tunes of romance,

Now, I also have my daughter,

Competing with her mom,

In cultivating her musical talents,

On the piano chords,

And I question,

Can heaven be any more glorious?

O, let the music flow,

And fill my hearth, with a joyous glow

Music is the universal language of love. Surround yourself with good quality music and let it enrich your heart and soul.

15-Marriage is not a prison cell. Allow each other a little breathing room and time to separately enjoy your own friends, sports, hobbies, cultural or professional associations.

For some thirty-five years, unfortunately, I have abused this privilege. I started early. Three days into our honeymoon, vacationing and having a good time in a gifted condominium on the beaches of Carmel in northern California, I had the stupidity of telling my wife, tsakoug (honey), that I had a meeting to go to, so I cut my honeymoon short and came to an Armenian National Committee meeting. At the time, Deukemejian was running for attorney general, and I was the treasurer of the committee in Northern California to elect him. Somehow, donating 15 to 20% of my time to political, cultural, religious, professional, and educational organizations was a sacred duty for me, and attending three to four meetings per week at night had been the norm. This was all when my wife and kids needed me the most. I learned too late that, even though I was devoting my time to good causes, it was not solely my time anymore. It was my wife's time, my son's time, my daughter's time.

So, having a little separate time is healthy, but please do not be as stupid as I was. Spending time with your family is the most important thing in life.

16-A wife's intelligence and sixth sense.

When I was in high school, I remember writing a three-page article in the school's monthly magazine about how the female brain was 200 grams smaller than the male brain, and wrote a lengthy dissertation about how, generally speaking, males were more intelligent. I remember my single Armenian studies male teacher, who was in his sixties and in charge of the publication, praised my insight and courage to write about a subject like this. Well, some forty years afterwards, I realized how wrong and naïve I was.

The truth is, ladies, or in this case, wives, have a sixth sense; their radar system works a lot better than ours as men. They see things we do not see, they can connect various seemingly unimportant dots and facts together, and their memory of events, dates, relationships and how to organize all that information is way superior. They can sniff and caution you from approaching pitfalls.

Unfortunately, it took me a long time to tap into this. In my mind, I was the banker, I was the finance major, I was the "smart" one in our marriage, and I felt, why should I consult my wife on business matters? The truth is, I would not have survived the down cycles of life without my wife's sixth sense, dogged determination and intelligence.

A word of advice, Garo, consult Lara when you are making important decisions. It's free, and I can assure, you will see and feel the positive effects.

17-Being number one for each other.

We all have a past. Both of you have had relationships in the past. Starting today, both of you have to know, have to feel, and have to trust that you are number one for each other. All other relationships become secondary. A wife or a husband can never be a second-fiddle position. It doesn't work; you have to be number one for each other.

Before I got married, I used to sing in a choir as well as dance with the San Francisco Armenian Hamazkayin dance group. We were made up of six very handsome young men and six fabulous-looking Armenian ladies. I was 165 pounds, with kind of dashing, long Beatle-lookalike hair, with a fluffy red shirt, baggy black trousers, and knee-high, very flexible boots to allow maximum flexibility for Armenian aerobatic dances. Of course, we had various pictures from our performances together as a group. One day, I come home, and I see Esther going through my albums with a pair of scissors, so I ask, "Tsakoug, what are you doing?" She answers, "I am making a collage of all your dance positions." I asked, "What's happening to the girls in the picture" to which she replied, "They volunteered to leave," and pointed to the adjacent waste basket.

So, sometimes, you have to defend your number one priority position and press a delete button.

18-Children and grandchildren

Bearing children brings fulfilment to our lives. It gives us an opportunity to participate in the continuation of God's creation. It gives a reward to our daily running around and hard work, and finally, it teaches us to love more than we love ourselves.

When my kids were born, I was too young and had lofty plans, a world to conquer. My parents were with me, so I felt safe that my children were getting the necessary care, attention, and love. I used to watch my dad and get tremendous pleasure seeing him have so much fun with my son. Well, now, my turn has come. I never knew the extent of heavenly pleasure that a grandfather experiences when they play with their grandchildren. When I have a pillow fight with my grandson, Gabriel, in my bedroom and experience his childish heart, and full, genuine innocent laughter, there is absolutely nothing better than that in this world. Finally, finally, I have an opportunity to give my wife the same treatment she has been giving me. She is no longer number one for me; she is behind my grandson. As soon as I see my grandson Gabriel, my facial muscles relax, and I smile with deep joy. Esther does not have that effect on me anymore.

So, Garo and Lara, don't mess around. September is nine months away. Get to work. I need more number ones in my life.

19-A wife as a problem.

Garo, I heard that, you told Lara, "You are no longer your parents' problem; you are my problem." Well, let me tell you, my daughter has never been a problem for me; a pain in my butt may be, but never a problem. Granted, you became Lara's husband today, and I love you for that, but I am abdicating nothing here. Lara is my daughter and will continue to be my daughter until the day I die.

Still, I like what you said; only a guy with real balls will say something like that. It tells me you are dependable and in charge.

Let me actually tell you what you are getting as a wife. When Lara was about six, we were living in La Canada in a very expensive house. We were sitting in the family room, and Esther was feeding Hrag with Lara next to us. She said, "Mom, when you grow up, you can give this house to Shahe, but give your dresses and hats to me, and I will take care of Hrag when you pass away." She knew that Hrag needed twenty-four hours of daycare, and she was willing to do that. She was only six, and nobody taught her to be that responsible and noble. She just has such a rare, caring, and loving heart; that's what you are getting; you are not getting a problem, but rather, your lottery ticket. just won the most amazing prize. Enjoy her.

And finally,

20-A couple of important "do not's" to assure long and happy marriage:

Do not smoke.

Do not drink

Do not gamble and

Do not screw around.

As I ponder here, Garo, your name is my brother's name. Your last name Atachian means "fire-ian." My second son that I lost was Hrag, which also means fire; maybe this way the Lord has put you in Lara's life and my family's life as a replacement for the son I lost. We are combining Atachian and Assilian, which means genuine fire, and we are going to have genuine fire grandchildren. I can't wait.

I know that you are going to tell me that this is so complicated and difficult; how are you going to do all this? Well, it will not be easy. I hope nobody told you that it is a picnic, and it requires a lot of commitment. You already said "I do" in front of all of us, and you are already in the tunnel. Remember, only 5% of marriages live long enough to celebrate their fiftieth anniversary. I am already 75% there, and I hope you both will be there too.

Tomorrow, when you wake up, the process of becoming a new person will start.

You now have a purpose in life,

You now have a reason to wake up,

Life itself will have a different meaning for you,

You now will discover Love, which is the main attribute of our Creator.

This is a new beginning in your life. A new year will be starting for all of us within twenty-four hours. This is a gift that the Lord has given you. You have your family's blessings, love, and support to form a new family. Love each other, enjoy each other, and let God's love glow in both of your faces for the rest of your days.

Merry Christmas and Happy New Year to all of you, and thank you again for participating in this joyous occasion.

MY DARLING DAUGHTER

Time flies so fast,

Sometimes I hate the speed

How fast have you grown?

How fast have you passed your mom's height?

My little girl of yesterday,

My little annoying, hot-headed, debate-loving girl,

Who could be so charming, pleasant, and loving,

Suddenly has become a lady.

And darling, even though you don't see it yet,

I know what a jewel you will be,

Especially with God at the center of your heart.

Happiness is stored for your life,

Take your time,

Enjoy your days;

You do not have to go high speed anywhere,

Do what you do most and best,

Love your family, your friends, and relatives,

And above all, just continue loving the Lord,

Everything else will just fall in place.

Shahe and lara

AN OPEN APPEAL TO MY SON & DAUGHTER

Anytime,

Anyplace,

You need my help,

You need my time,

For my grandchildren,

I will pause and drop everything I am doing,

And I will be there.

It does not matter what I am doing at the time,

How important or urgent the matter is that I am occupied with,

I will drop it immediately and be there when you need me,

My grandchildren are first priority for me,

Nothing, and no one, is ahead of them,

When you need me to help my grandchildren,

I will be there,

Anytime and anyplace,

So, help me, God.

My wife, in practice, performs this love affair towards our grandchildren

Better than I do.

A PLAYFUL LITTLE KITTEN

I noticed a playful little kitten tumbling in between my two feet.

I watched her with a smile on my face,

Such a cute little cute loveable creature.

Suddenly, a much bigger, angry cat approached my little kitten,

And started harassing and scaring my little friend.

I tried to push the big cat way,

But it wouldn't budge and it started a ferocious attack on the cute little kitten.

So, I started kicking the big cat to leave my little kitten alone,

Until I heard "Ayy!" from my wife.

I woke up and noticed my wife was sleeping next to me.

I realized I was just dreaming about the cats and

Hit my wife in my sleep. That was the first time I raised my hand on my wife,

In forty-one years of marriage.

And it happened when I was dreaming.

I sincerely apologized and went back to sleep.

When we woke up a few hours later, I apologized again

For unintentionally hitting her.

She had no idea what I was talking about.

If anyone, who like Joseph or Daniel

Can explain this dream,

I would be very grateful.

We can talk about half my kingdom later on,

Besides, I am allergic to cats,

My eyes get irritated and watery,

And I do not necessarily enjoy having cats around.

Rubbing their body on my feet and leaving their hair on my pants.

Go figure.

LOVE HAS TO BE FREE

Do not pay for love,

Once you do, it will have no value.

Love has to be free,

No price tag attached,

No material conditions imposed,

No financial expectations anticipated.

Love overflowing from the heart is priceless,

Once you see material things attached to love,

Run away from it.

To find pure love,

You have to nurture it in yourself first.

INDESCRIBABLE LOVE SONG

From the deepest corners of my hectic mind,

The tenderest part of my thirsty soul,

The sweetest words of my rustic pen,

Merge together and let a mellow song of love,

Describe the happiness I am in.

TO MY WIFE

The best way I know how to relate to my wife,

Is to realize how blessed I am.

The Lord has been very generous with me,

To give me a wife who has been

Such a crucial support for thirty-five years.

I thought I was independent,

I thought I was strong,

I thought I was smart,

I thought I was a hard worker,

Until I met my match.

Who time and time again,

Humbles me with her strength and energy.

When I am weak and burdened with tremendous worries,

She picks me up with her unshakeable reservoir of faith

Pulls me up and pushes me forward.

Time and time again,

When I fall while facing life's battles,

She is there with her steadfast resolve,

To retrieve me,

Yet I look at her fragile, graceful size

With adoration and pride.

Where does she pack all that strength?

Where does she pack all that energy?

She is my wife, my prize, my trophy

My best gift from God, who must have loved me,

To give me such a wife,

My wish and prayer

O my lord

Is to be a deserving husband

To my wife.

SNAPSHOT CLICKS

A click here, a click there,

Snapshots of past moments in time,

Makes me realize that time is clicking away and turning to memories.

Some friends, relatives in those snapshots,

Have already departed.

You reflect in sadness and gratitude,

That you are still here.

You remember the location, the time, the circumstances,

Then look at the mirror.

All those snapshots of the past have changed your appearance.

You do not look the same anymore, you have changed, aged, and matured.

Well, it all depends on your perspective,

Pictures are a reflection of physical reality,

They do not lie.

Physically, we might not look the same anymore,

But, mentally, spiritually, culturally, intellectually, and knowledge-
wise,

All characteristics that do not come out in the snapshots,

Hopefully will provide a lot of comforts and positive affirmation,

That, what can I say,

We are mentally at ease and comfortable

With the whole snapshot clicking process.

A FEAST TO THE EYE

My MBA thesis prior to graduation from San Francisco State
University

Was a comparative analysis of American and Japanese banking
systems,

Comparing the thirteen Japanese largest City banks

With that of the thirteen largest US banks.

As such, in the middle of my banking career,

Wells Fargo Bank put me in charge of the bank's relationships

With all Japanese banks and corporations from the head office in
San Francisco.

At the time, Japan was the second largest economy in the world
behind the US

And Japanese presence and investments in the US and California
was substantial and widespread

In the fields of automobiles, banking, electronics, real estate, steel,
and natural resources.

It was during this time that I got introduced to delicate Japanese
cuisine.

In California we have a wide range of international cuisine.

The Japanese cuisine, however, stands out with their primary
emphasis on

Feasting the eye first.

The way they present their dishes,

With so much attention to detail, artistic color coordination of bites,

Sculpturing with their sharp knives exquisite sushi art pieces on a plate,

That you look upon with so much admiration and appreciation,

For the time and effort the chef has put just for you,

To entice and please your eyes,

Before it conquers your mouth watering taste buds.

Once you treat yourself to this elegance,

You will not have a desire to come down from that elevation.

All these out of context thoughts came to my mind, while I was sitting at church,

(Maybe I was getting hungry)

I was watching my wife walk up the podium towards the organ,

Then she came down elegantly towards the piano on the right.

I gazed in amazement to her floral fitted dress,

The cautious but firm steps she took, her hairdo, her shoes, her necklace,

Were all coordinated and pleasant,

The way she felt and expressed the music she was playing,

With her overall body language,

The style, presentation, and her appearance,

And all of these feelings,

Was circulating in my mind, forty-eight years after we have been married,

It was all, a feast to my eye,

A feast to my senses,

That I will cherish with a thankful heart to the Almighty.

A STATE OF SOLITUDE

My wife is attending a women's retreat this three-day weekend in
San Luis Obispo.

We take each other for granted after forty years.

It is very odd for me to go to sleep and wake up without my wife.

Come back home,

Kind of lonely, all by myself,

I'm glad it's only one more night and she will be home,

Sometimes it takes a state of solitude

To realize the real power of your wife over you.

SHE IS

She is my busy bee,

She is my pride,

She is my life's prize,

She is a comforter to all my anxieties,

She is my love,

She is my reason for waking up,

She is music to my soul,

She is a beauty inside and out,

She is the mother to my children,

And even a better grandmother to my grandchildren.

She is righteous to the bone,

There are no gray areas in her mind,

Either right or wrong, very simple, nothing in between,

She abstains and abhors wrong paths,

Years pass by with such grace on her face,

She is kind and considerate to so many,

She spreads love all around,

And she is the definition of graceful.

After all,

She is my queen, Esther.

Hoover Dam in late 70s

LOVE IS . . .

Love is making the Lord the center of your family,

Because,

He is the best definition of love,

HE IS LOVE.

Love is knowing the difference between what is right

And what is wrong,

And abstaining from wrong acts,

Love is loving when your loved one has no capacity to love back.

Love can not be bought with money or material things.

Love is never a perfect match, but rather a constant practice of compromise,

Love is being faithful, truthful, loyal,

Love is being the first to say sorry,

Love is to forgive once, twice, and as often as needed,

Love is to have the courage to say no to temptations,

Love is to think of your loved one before you think of yourself,

Love is to argue, and not mind losing the argument, even if you think you are right,

Love is to have goosebumps, by your lover's touch,

Love is feeling a natural relaxation of your facial muscles simply by seeing your loved one,

Love is feeling happy, simply by making your loved one happy,

Love is holding, embracing, squeezing your loved one,

Love is feeling inner comfort by simply holding her hand,

Love is getting a surge of energy by her mere presence,

Love is feeling lonely and dysfunctional when she goes away for a few days,

Love is looking, gazing, appreciating, and enjoying,

The apparent and hidden inside beauty of your loved one,

Love is feeling so lucky for the prize you have been given,

Love is the ability to truthfully call your wife your better half

After forty-one years of marriage and mean it.

Love is calling the decision to marry your wife

The best decision you have made in life.

Love, is holding her body tightly against yours,

Knowing full well that you are in the meadows of heaven.

Finding real love is a blessing from God,

But, you have to discover it deep in your heart first.

It is never too late,

Start today.

PLANTING MY PEARLS

I've liked freestyle poetry since I was young,

I always looked at it as a distilled and meaningful medium,

Of expressing thoughts, emotions and feelings.

Even though I always have a specific audience in mind,

I would never know,

Who and when?

What I write?

Will be read,

Or, if it will ever have an impact or relevance on any human soul?

I definitely wanted to leave an imprint behind me;

I definitely wanted to talk about subjects

That can sustain the test of time.

As I have gone through my life's journey,

The continuously happy and successful years,

Together with the difficult, draining, and dark years,

The key messages I want to convey:

Is first, a message of faith,

Faith in God and a deep inner desire to feel His presence,

In your own life,

And the resulting peace, harmony, and comfort,

That holy experience will generate.

The second key message is that of hope,

Hope, that no matter how difficult our circumstances happen to be,

We can always depend on hope

Tomorrow will be a better day.

Hope in life,

Hope in the fairness and the goodness of God,

That can see us through all our life's valleys.

And finally, the last message is that of love,

God is love,

Our world will make no sense without love,

LOVE, IS THE FOUNDATION,

AROUND WHICH WE CAN ANCHOR OUR LIVES.

MAY GOD'S LOVE AND PEACE BE WITH YOU, FOR THE REST OF YOUR DAYS.

Made in the USA
Middletown, DE
10 April 2023

28472617R00186